AF490546

FEEDLOTS, RANCHES AND ROPIN'

DENNIS H. WILLIAMS

For information contact: info@outlawspublishing.com
2024 Revision by Michael Clement
Cover design by Outlaws Publishing.
Published by Outlaws Publishing.
December 2024
10 9 8 7 6 5 4 3 2 1

Note From the Author

The contents of this book are 40 years of working in the livestock industry. I've been involved in just about every phase of the Cattle Industry with working in feedlots, on ranches, and even 16 months in a large packing house. Along with this is a lifetime of rodeoing and jackpot ropings. The sorties told here are short snippets of the day-to-day work and the people we worked for. I tried to maintain the vocabulary and the flavor of the day, so I hope the reader finds more entertainment here. I sure had fun writing it! A lot of the stuff here deals with the great cowboys and cowgirls I've crossed paths with… without them, I wouldn't have anything to say. Enjoy!

In the preparation of this book, there are a few people to thank:

The Verde Girls -Annette, Michelle, and Debbie -Thanks for your support

My lifelong friend, John, whose moral support is greatly appreciated.

The hard work and patience of Stephanie, who did the proof-reading and corrections, and liaison work

And, lastly, Mrs. Jefe, who raised three children in a world of drugs, alcohol, and still turned out quality people. All the while tolerating the whims of a heavily addicted cowpuncher.

FEEDLOTS

Black Eye

Years ago, when I was workin' at a now-defunct feedlot, there was a guy there who was always in Dutch with his wife. He was great; she was great; but one beer together, and it was war!

One day, he came to work with a black eye.

"What happened?" we all asked.

"She gave it to me when she was doin' the laundry," he said.

"Why?" we asked.

"Yesterday, when we was markin' those steers with that red markin' chalk, I got some on my hands. Then it rubbed off on my underwear when I went to pee. She saw the red chalk and thought it was lipstick. Then she gave me the eye!"

Which Horse Was Most Efficient

Years ago, when I was a button, I was workin' for a feed yard run by a sure 'nuff real-deal cowboy-cowman. We saddled up at 3:30, summer or winter.

I was catchin' my pony one mornin' when Sam was showin' the new man his horses by the light of a single danglin' light bulb. This fella had a pair of Gene Autry bat-wing chaps, a pair of Buffalo Bill gauntlets, and a wire-brim J.C. Penney felt hat.

I heard Sam groan as the guy asked, "Which horse is the most efficient?"

Jack the Coffee Thief

Years ago, when I was the cow boss at a now-defunct feed yard, there was a little guy who worked there who reminded me of a yappin' little lapdog that peed on everything. We also had a gal pen rider who was damn good and tough.

We all brought our coffee in thermoses for a break mid-mornin'. The gal always brought flavored coffee, and Jack would sneak in and drink it when she wasn't lookin'.

One day, when she came to work, she put her thermos in the usual place and warned us all not to touch it.

Later that mornin', we saw Jack sneak into the saddle room and sample the coffee. Didn't see him no more for three days. She'd doctored it with Ex-Lax and Croton Oil!

Cow Bell for the New Bride

Years ago, when I was a button, I was workin' for an outfit that had a head cowboy who got married. He had been quite a ladies' man, so a friend of mine and I got into their house before they came home from the wedding.

To the bed springs, we hung a cowbell.

The new bride didn't come out of the house for a week, and the groom wouldn't speak to any of us for two days!

Barry 'Baby' Brashears

Here's one for you Verde Valley folks that know Barry "Baby" Brashears. Years ago, he and another puncher were workin' for me in a feed yard. The rule was: no ropin' for fun. The boss was death on it. As a matter of fact, he had put the word out that the next one he caught was history.

Barry, Kim, and me were in a pen ropin' on a Saturday evenin' when the boss called on the two-way, wantin' me in the office. I loped up there and tied my horse outside.

When we finished what we had to do, the boss asked me to take his Blazer and gas it up. I could see the boys ropin', so I idled down close, then gunned the engine and spun tires all the way to them.

Ropes flew outta the pen every which way.

I was smilin' as I cruised by! The boys weren't happy.

Old Hoot

Old Hoot was a hell of an old cowboy, but as time overtook him, he became an alcoholic with no bounds.

We tolerated him as long as he was halfway sober, but more than half the time, we sent him home.

One mornin', shippin' fat cattle, it was an hour before daylight, but we had a big yeller moon. Four of us went into the pen to drive the steers to the gate and into the alley, but only three of us went out the gate.

We turned back to see Hoot drivin' his own shadow down the fence, cussin' it for not goin' out the gate!

Hoot went home that day.

Young and Reckless

When I was young and reckless, I was workin' at a now-defunct feedlot that had a poor attitude toward cowboys.

We were shippin' fat cattle one mornin' in the rain. I was in the lead, in the dark, with a poncho over my head in a drivin' rain. Ole Chickin, the long-legged horse I was ridin', pulled the plug in the middle of about two feet of mud and manure. The first jump, my knees were in the seat of my saddle. Ole Chick bucked on down the alley, but as I struggled to my feet, he ran over me again, goin' the other way. As I got up, he came over me again. This happened four or five times until that bunch of idiots behind me figured out there was a gate shut in front of me, and they finally caught the horse!!

Last Feedlot

Years ago, when I was a button, I went to work at the last feedlot in Phoenix. It was bordered by 48th Street on the west, Washington on the north, with the Salt River on the south. There were two old punchers who had been there since Noah unloaded the boat.

Buster was a big man and kinda quiet. Homer Lee was about five feet tall and could talk a blue streak. The sensitive noses in the neighborhood complained about the smell, so the owners put in a mister system along 48th that put out a perfume.

The first mornin' it was workin', we all were ridin' along the line. Homer went to wavin' his hand in front of his face, "Wh-wh-ew, my wife will think I smell like a whorehouse." Without lookin' up, Buster mumbled, "How would your wife know what a whorehouse smelled like?"

The fight was on!!!

No Pencil

Years ago, I went to work for a large feedlot with 60 thousand head as a pen rider. After I'd been there a couple of weeks, the super drove up in his pickup.

"GO DOWN TO PEN SO-AND-SO AND GIVE ME A HEAD COUNT, AND WRITE IT DOWN."

I told the old man I had no pencil, but I could write it down on my Copenhagen can if I had one. He opened the glove box and pulled out a new box of Eagle pencils.

Handing me one, he told me, "Cut off what you need and give me the rest back!!!"

I carried that stub of pencil the whole time I worked there—in my hatband!!

Breezy

Breezy had a temper, and it showed up one cold January mornin'. We had stopped at the scale house and got a cup of Joe to warm up a bit. The super made a wiseass remark about us not bein' good enough to be inside, so we took our cups of coffee with us and left.

Breezy's horse was a little blue roan called Tiger who, the more you fussed with him, jigged and acted up. The alley was knee-deep in mud and muck. We were easin' along, tryin' not to spatter each other, when Tiger started cuttin' up.

Breezy was already mad from what the super said, so he just poured that cup of hot coffee down ole Tiger's ear!!!!

So much for stayin' clean!!!

Purple Continental

In the '70s and '80s, it was good economic practice for people with lots of money to invest in feedlot cattle. A black comedian was a big plunger, as long as the cattle were black. With the rage on in Angus cattle, I'd say he knew somethin'.

Mike and I were workin' at a now-defunct feedlot when, on a Saturday mornin' before daylight, we could hear a radio playin' down in the pens. As it got light, we ambled down into the yard.

In a pen of fat cattle was a purple Continental stuck in a mud hole. The doors were open, fat steers rubbin' on the car, brushin' up against it and knockin' dents into it.

As we got closer, we could see whiskey bottles scattered around and feet stickin' out of the car's front and back seats. A little closer, and we realized it was a couple of popular movie stars. I won't use their names because one is still with us.

Turns out, they were lookin' for their cattle.

We got a tractor to pull the car to dry land, and the yard boss took those two cattle barons to the airport.

So ends that episode, never to return those two!!

Anson

Anson was a big ole kid, kinda slow, but willing as all get out. He liked to rope, and his summer job at the feedlot fit right in.

He had a big ole platter-footed horse that couldn't run fast enough to scatter his own droppings with a rake tied to his tail!!!

We were practicin' one afternoon after work when Anson decided to help the chute help move a steer up into the roping chute. But instead of gettin' off his horse, he hung his rope with a loop built over the saddle horn and leaned over the side to nudge the steer.

Just as he was leanin' off the side of his horse, the header called for the steer!

Three horses left in pursuit of the steer—the header, the heeler, and ole platter-foot—with Anson's foot hung in that big loop!!!

Anson's fanny was plowing a furrow down the arena you could plant corn in!! W hen we got ole platter-foot stopped, Anson got up, kicked the horse in the butt and said, "why can't you run that fast when I'm on your back!!"

I Buy Ya Beer and Pay Ya to Drink It

When I was the yard boss at the Spur Feedlot in San Tan, Arizona, we had a real wet winter goin' on. It had rained so much, the corrals were knee-deep in mud and slop. We had a full house, with more cattle comin' in every night. Many times, the cattle that came in stood in an alley all night until we emptied a corral of fat cattle the next mornin'. For six weeks, we were at a long trot from before daylight to after dark—and sometimes later.

The superintendent was a young man, freshly married and just outta college. Unlike most in his position, he was a great guy and handled pressure like a pro. We'd hired a couple of day laborers to help with the increasing load—sick cattle, fat cattle to sort, and thousands to process and brand.

One of the few sunshiny days we'd had, the super came by where I was sortin' fats. He said, "I'm gonna buy us a case of beer, and tonight, I don't care what needs doin'—everyone be at the saddle house at five. We're gonna have a beer."

I spread the word, and everyone perked up a little! Sure enough, at five o'clock, Jr. drove up with a case of beer. He even passed it out to everyone and, with a smile, told us what a great job we were doin' and thanked us for our devotion to duty.

Now, the regular crew was salaried, but the two day men were paid by the hour. After the second round, Jr. looked at the day men and asked, "Did you dock out?"

They smiled and shook their heads. Jr. dropped his beer and ran into the saddle room, where we heard the dock bang twice. As he came out, he said, "Damn, I buy ya beer and pay ya to drink it!!!"

It was a good time. Little did we know, a month later, Jr. and his wife would be dead in a plane wreck while on a Christmas vacation and honeymoon. We sure missed him—a great guy.

A Bank and a Steer

Well, here's a cowboy story that was requested by the blonde bomber.

Years ago, at the Phoenix stockyards, a bank was built to accommodate the cattle feeders and the livestock industry in general. It sat on the corner of 48th and Washington, in a big ol' lot that used to be cattle pens. It was paved and open to the world.

This was in the days before shatterproof glass, and this bank had giant plate glass windows along the front. Well, as in most cattle situations, there were cattle crawlin' outta the feedlot and wanderin' around the neighborhood. We very seldom had cattle go as far as the bank, the stockyard's restaurant, or the set of office buildings that made up the cattlemen's complex.

The bank manager was a self-righteous S.O.B. who thought us workin', shit-kickin' punchers were less than human.

One day, just before noon, the feed truck informed us that a steer was wanderin' around the complex and asked if we could catch him before that banker called the boss. We struck a trot up that way; it wasn't far.

Well, this particular steer was a chronic offender when it came to gettin' out and visitin' the neighborhood. Cattle like that usually got a dose of nylon rope injected by a strong right arm on a big stout horse.

This particular steer had already received that treatment a time or two, so when he saw us comin', he decided to make himself scarce!

When he trotted past the front of the bank, he saw his own reflection in that big plate glass window and just naturally thought he should hide with that steer! He jumped through that window right into the bank lobby!!

When we got there, the tellers were up on the counters, and that pompous banker was pleadin' for someone to come help and to "bring someone with them!!!" I slipped in a foot, roped ole steer, and handed the rope to a man outside, who led him out.

You know, there wasn't a speck of cow shit in that bank!

Smokey

When I worked at Arizona Land and Cattle, they had cattle interests all over Arizona, Colorado, and New Mexico. One of their outfits was an alfalfa pasture and growing yard in Florence, Arizona.

The man takin' care of it up and quit, and there was no one left to look after things. It was about twenty miles from where I was, so I got elected to drive down and take care of the cattle until a new man could be hired.

The alfalfa fields were fenced in with electric fencing, so someone had to be there every day. I didn't need to take a horse, as Smokey had left a good string there. Him being' renowned for making' good horses, I knew I would be mounted well the first day I caught a good bay to ride. Man, he was nice—traveled good, was gentle, and when I tried out ropin' a pinkeye steer, you couldn't have asked for a better mount. As I was ridin' in that afternoon, a little piece of baling wire flipped out of the weeds, and ole bay stampeded! He ran about 100 yards before I got him stopped.

As time went on, I found that every horse there would do that if a wire or string brushed up against their leg, yet they were all good to shoe and gentle to work around. A few years later, I ran into a feller who worked for Smokey there, and I asked what caused those good horses to act so. He said, "When Smokey wanted to test the electric fence, he was always forgetting' the tester, so he'd just back his horse into it to see if it was hot!!!"

One Steer Standing

Years ago, when I worked for the new Tovrea feed yard in Maricopa, we were rollin'. The Swift packing plant in Tolleson had opened up and was killing' cattle at an amazing' rate for that day and time. The trucking industry in Arizona wasn't prepared for the onslaught, so every conceivable kind of truck was pressed into service. Most were truck-and-pull trailers, single-deck with plywood sides held together with cable!! You talk about scary—40 head of fat cattle goin' down the road weavin' back and forth. Spooky!

One mornin', I was loadin' one of 15 or 20 trucks headed to Tolleson. Two trucks had already left, loaded. Suddenly, the scale house door flew open, and the boss ran out, jumped in his truck, spun around, and headed down the road like his tail was on fire! Behind him, the other three cowboys jumped on their horses and left at a lope, yellin' at me to come when I got done. I asked, "Where?" They pointed to where the road crossed the train tracks.

I looked that way and saw one steer standing' on a trailer with no sideboards—the truck was nowhere in sight. Back then, there weren't crossing' arms on the track, so a sleepy-headed driver had pulled in front of a train. The train hit where the truck and trailer coupled. The truck kept moving' but lost the boards on the tail end. The shock of the collision shattered the boards on the trailer, killing' all the cattle but one. By the time I got there, that steer was still standing' on the naked trailer, and the driver was froze to the wheel!!

Last Train Load

In the early '70s, I had the privilege of working' for a feed yard that probably took delivery of the last trainload of cattle in that manner. When they built this feed yard, they installed a rail siding, which, to my knowledge, was used just this once.

These cattle came directly out of Mexico—also an unheard-of thing for that day and time. As I remember, there were 38 forty-foot cars, each packed with between 40 and 60 head. The bulls were tied in the corners with inch-thick cotton rope, as was the custom of the day. Being the youngest (and dumbest), it fell to me that when a car was spotted at the chute, I would slide the door open, climb the inside wall, and walk around it to push the cattle out. Anything tied, I'd untie and get them out.

Now, a Mexican bull tied up in a corner for 48 hours ain't a happy camper!! There's not near as much room in those cars as one might think! By the end of it, the legs of my Wranglers were shredded. Sometimes, the bulls didn't want to leave the car, so who do you think got elected to tease the animal into charging down the chute? Yup—ol' dumb shit!

We finished unloading' in the dark, with no lights, and it was a full mile to the scales. Everyone's horses were pooped, and so were we. This trainload of cattle had been pieced together in Mexico in small bunches, so there was every kind of critter mixed in—from old work oxen with holes bored through their horns for driving' lines to six-month-old calves. We sorted for days, then spent another week brandin' them through the squeeze chute.

I could be wrong, but I believe this was the one and only trainload of cattle unloaded there—and possibly the last one in Arizona.

T&C Cattle Co

When I got out of high school and was going' to college part time, I worked for the Tovrea feedlots under the name T&C Cattle Co. When I learned the boss was leaving', I decided I didn't want to stay either.

I had a little socked away: a new pickup and a single-horse trailer with a fair kinda head horse. After takin' the summer off, I figured I needed a job. Another feedlot came callin' on a Sunday morning'. I went to work on Monday. In those days, everything I owned fit in the camper on the pickup and the saddle compartment of that trailer, so the move was easy.

For six years at Tovreas, every animal that was sick was roped and doctored. If he weighed 1400 or 200, he got roped! No squeeze chute doctorin' there, but when ropin' the cattle, they weren't rodeoed either. I've helped doctor 25 head of calves out of 100 in a corral, roped everyone, and NEVER got an animal out of a walk. We were just a level above most other feedlots.

At the new feedlot, cowboys weren't allowed to use a rope. Most didn't even carry one. My second day there, we were coming' up a feed alley when we found a big fat steer upside-down in the feed bunk. In his pickup, there was the super. I was the only cowboy there with a rope. The super pointed to me and told me to pull that steer out.

"No," I told him. "When you hired me, you told me I'd get fired for takin' that rope down. Pull the steer out, and I'll never say a word to you!"

I pulled the steer out, and over the next three years I worked there, I could rope whatever NEEDED roping and never a word was said. But during those three years, he fired three or four men just for swingin' a rope while driving cattle down an alley!

Pancho

PANCHO was a Mexican cowboy at Hughes and Ganz feed yard. He'd been there since it was built before, actually, as he was irrigating the land when the feedlot was built. He was a little thick in the middle, didn't speak very plain English, rode a Montgomery Ward saddle, and used a Jap-made bit on all his horses, but make no mistake, he was all cowboy.

One of his horses was a big, feather-legged ole pony that was black, bald-faced, and stockin'-legged. Maybe somewhere his ancestor pulled a plow, but that ole pony was a cow horse, especially when Pancho rode him. Now that ole pony was gentle, but he wouldn't tolerate no foolishness.

One mornin', while it was still dark and Pancho was sippin' coffee in the scale house, three of us saddled the ole baldy with the saddle on backwards! It was a fight, and it took all three of us to do it. When Pancho saw this, he grinned and shook his head, but that was all.

One of the guys, who was the ringleader in this little prank, was a pickup driver boss. The next day, the keys to his pickup were gone. We searched high and low, but no keys. He had to get a new ignition set for the truck.

In the scale house, there was a mounted steer head with a big set of horns. One day, while sittin' there with a cup of coffee, I happened to look up at that head. A set of keys hung from one horn.

Wonder how that happened?

Pancho only smiled!!

Working Cattle in the Glades

Not long ago, I commented in a post about an outfit I worked for having a ranch in Florida and the cattle coming' out of the trucks with gators snappin' at their heels. Here's the story:

When I had just gone to work for AZL, they'd bought a 3,000-head ranch in Florida. Why they felt they needed the cattle in Arizona, I don't know, but as the cracker cowboys put a load together, they put wheels under 'em, smoke over 'em, and sent them swamp angels west. By the time they hit the ground in Queen Creek, Arizona, they were for sure ringy. A lot of those cattle hadn't been gathered in years, and they were sure upset to lose their homes in the palmetto forests. Very few would drink out of a trough or were safe to walk through a foot of water, as the water trough washer found out.

These cattle were all over 800 pounds on arrival, after a 2,000-mile trip, so it took 'em a few days to recover, then there was hell amongst the yearlings. A feed truck would drive by, and they all crashed into the fences at the back side of the corrals. When a pen rider went into the pen, he had to pay attention to where he was at all times. If something' startled those suckers, you could get run over big time. They didn't look where they were going' when they ran.

After about six months, the company higher-ups decided it must be the poor help in Florida—what with poppin' them whips and all—that made the cattle like that. So, they hired a bunch of sure enough Arizona cowpunchers and sent a manager from Queen Creek there to show the crackers how to do it. Well, the manager stayed, but them Arizona punchers came home in six weeks. "Them people are nuts," they told me. It wasn't people makin' 'em cattle crazy, it was the gators, the skeeters, heel flies, and worst of all, the damn hurricanes.

Old Scooter

Old Scooter was a plain ol' sorrel pony that had spent his whole life in the stockyards in Phoenix working' for the Tavera family. He was sure-footed, stout on a rope, and could cut a cow with the best of 'em. He had one problem: he didn't like needles—not one bit. I've seen unsuspecting fellows walk into his stall with a needle in hand and escape with their lives! I know, I was one! When it came time to give Scooter a shot, you went into the stall with a bridle, then blindfolded him, hobbled him, twisted an ear, and you MIGHT give him the shot!! But, with that, he was a great cow pony. And, in a pinch, you could haul him to a ropin' and be competitive!

Clayton was the cattle buyer for Tavera, and very seldom got horseback, but would on occasion. It had rained steady for a week. The pens were ankle-deep in soup, and slick as ice under the soup. We all had been down at least once as it was just scary as hell in those pens. Those old pens didn't have alleys to sort in, so three men would hold the cattle at one end of a corral while the boss would cut the fats out past you. Then when he had enough, we'd put the cuts in the feed alley and drive 'em to the scales.

When Clayton came to sort, he always borrowed ol' Scooter. In the trunk of the Cadillac he drove, he carried a handmade Van Core saddle, two Navajo blankets, and a Salinas-ported Garcia bit on a filigreed headstall. Ol' Scooter looked like a showboat with all that hoss jewelry. We were sorting some fats one day after the rain let up. Clayton, for all his loud talk, fancy outfit, and cigar smokin', was a top hand. We'd sorted 20 head or so, all of us puckered up with our saddle seats halfway up our rectums, when Clayton started a big ol' crossbred steer. No matter what we did, we couldn't get out of the way enough for Clayton to put that steer outta the herd. After the third or fourth dash across the pen, ol' Scooter had enough. He put his shoulder into that steer, bit him in the neck, and they ran along together to the feed bunk with Clayton's face as white as a bed sheet. When they got to the feed bunk, Scooter jumped up on the concrete apron and slid with all four feet locked up!! The steer went down, then turned and trotted to the cuts. Clayton had bit his cigar in two and was froze to the saddle horn like death on a grim cowpuncher. Under his breath, we heard him say, "You damned old scrub… cow when I tell ya to cow!"

Kosher Buyer

The cattle market was in the tank. I know, what's new? But this was the early '70s, and AZL was trying to get rid of too many cattle that cost too much, were eating their heads off, and the packers didn't want them at any price. I had sorted one set of Angus steers so many times that my wife started threatening to send me to the couch if I called her by name in my sleep one more time!

We were down to the last four truckloads of steers in a particular lot. There wasn't a nickel's worth of difference in any of them. They were too light, still eating more than they could gain, and the packer buyers still looked the other way when they drove by. I had, at the request of the fat seller, re-sorted for the third or fourth time before we went to lunch.

When I came back an hour later, the seller was waiting at the saddle house. He'd shown this bunch of overfed midgets to a potential kosher buyer during lunch, and the buyer said he'd take one certain pen if I would re-sort and shape them up. I almost fell over. I'd done everything but paint them pink! But the seller insisted, couldn't I do *something*?

I told him I needed an hour to come up with something. After he left, I saddled my horse and went to the pens. I looked at the cattle in the pen the kosher buyer wanted and then at the other pen. Same cattle—no difference. In desperation, I switched the pens with the cattle.

That afternoon, the seller came around with a big smile on his face. "I don't know what you did," he said, "but the buyer liked them so much he bought the fronts and the tailender at two dollars more per head!" But they were the same cattle, I protested!

The seller just grinned. "The buyer thought no one could've sorted them any better!" From then on, I had to live up to that stunt as the best fat cattle sorter in Arizona! Out of the frying pan and into the fire!

Bone-Headed Stunt

While working at AZL, we would often turn lots of steers out on company ranches. Usually, we turned them out in October and hoped for winter rain to bring the desert back to life. But if it didn't rain, those cattle would starve unless you got them off. We often sent cattle to pasture, and in 60 days, they would come back lighter than when they left.

The ranch super—who was in charge of all the Arizona ranches—had a knack for making bone-headed decisions. This one fall, we had four thousand little Mexican steers all shaped up and ready to go as soon as the rains hit. Sure enough, in mid-October, it rained for four straight days. On the fifth day, we loaded the trucks and sent the little guys out to the desert. It was a big gamble, but the ranch super loved to take risks when he wasn't paying the bills.

Unfortunately, it didn't rain another drop. The green sprouted and then dried back to dusty, brown scrub. The ranch manager called me in a panic. He didn't have enough help to gather and ship those steers, but the super was making him hold them, hoping for more rain. The manager feared the steers would be too weak to survive a cold rain. Damned if you do, damned if you don't.

I sent four of my best men to that dust bowl ranch to help gather and ship the steers. It was twelve miles of dirt road to the headquarters, across an adobe flat that would choke you to death in the dust when dry, and bog a saddle blanket if it got wet.

On December 2nd, it started raining. The crew was stuck there for almost two weeks, fighting the weather and pulling weak steers out of mud holes. It rained for a week, then they got three days of sunshine, but the ground was still too wet to drive out. On the fourth day, the rain returned for another two days.

By the time I got my crew back, it was May, but the steers were a lot bigger than when they went out. I swore I would never send my cowboys out like that again. The workload back home had more than doubled for those who stayed behind.

Homer

Homer had spent his entire life at the Tovera stockyards. The only other job he'd had was serving in the Army during World War II. By the time I arrived, he was just a few weeks away from retirement. He was a character! His favorite mount was an old grey horse named Turdy, and every other horse he rode was dubbed Turdy, Jr. His horses were so fat that his legs stuck straight out from the sides of his saddle. He wasn't much over five feet tall and wore the biggest-brimmed hat he could find, chewing Day's Work plug tobacco. When he spat, he did it upwards, and it hit the brim of his hat before dribbling down into the wind, blowing right back into his face.

Year-round, whether summer or winter, he wore a Levi's jacket buttoned at the throat, with the rest of the buttons left undone. When it was cold and he complained about it, someone would suggest he button up his jacket. He'd simply say, "It wouldn't do no good no how!" The same response came in the summer when he complained about the heat and someone suggested he take the jacket off.

Despite all his quirks, Homer was a damn good cowboy. It was said that he could tell when a steer was about to get sick, even before the steer knew it. He roped well, always with a tied rope. Every month, he'd get a new rope, thanks to the company's account at the local livestock supply store. Homer made sure to grab his new rope on the first of every month, but his old ropes weren't wasted—they were often traded at the bar for whiskey.

One day, we were about to doctor a big, fat steer with an abscess on his ribs. We circled the steer a few times, trying to get a clean throw. The steer weighed about 1,400 pounds, and we all knew that whoever caught the head needed a good rope and a strong horse to keep things under control in the slick pens. Homer, as usual, was ready. The steer trotted by him and Turdy, and Homer cast his rope in front of the animal. He made a perfect catch.

But when the steer hit the end of the rope, everything went sideways. The steer was behind and alongside, and when those two forces hit, old Turdy did a handstand in front, his tail popped up behind, and Homer was launched like a rocket. He landed astride a cable fence and then fell into a water trough with his mouth open, no sound coming out.

We quickly freed Turdy and got Homer out of the trough. When he finally looked around, the only thing he said was, "That steer didn't need no attention!"

Rabies!!!

It had been a wet winter, and the feedlot at San Tan was full and knee-deep in mud. Cattle were coming and going daily as we processed and managed the health of untold numbers of cattle from every direction of the compass. When the southwestern Arizona deserts get rain, there's never enough cattle to eat all the grass.

Joe and I were taking care of a couple of long alleys of grass cattle—probably five thousand head. We were short-handed, short-tempered, and just plain tired. The boss and his wife had been killed in a plane wreck, and all the knowledge about those cattle was locked in his head. Joe and I had a good idea about a lot of them just from memory, but turns out, no one really knew for sure. If some random person had walked in and claimed they owned five hundred head, there would have been no way to prove it one way or another.

Every day, someone we didn't know called about their cattle and asked when they could go to grass. The girl in the office was completely stumped. A lot of these guys were partners in bunches of cattle, and the brands were leased from the company. Without some kind of paperwork, there was hardly any way to tell whose cattle were whose.

We started by tearing' apart the deceased boss's pickup. The keys had been in his pocket when he died, and no one knew where they had gone. After a couple of hours, we found a small tally book. It contained some transactions he had meant to record but hadn't gotten around to. Using this book, we began piecing together the owners and their cattle.

One particular string of cattle had come from Mexico and was a partnership deal with an especially obnoxious fellow and the company. This partner was an Okie car dealer, and he called daily, being a nuisance. He wanted those cattle on grass—and NOW. I had a couple of heated discussions with this guy, and almost daily, he had the office girl in tears. A new boss was coming, but it would be a month before he arrived. Joe and I had to hold it together as best we could.

One afternoon, as Joe and I were checking these Mexican-Okie partnership cattle, we noticed a brown steer running frantically from one end of the pen to the other, bawling like mad, running into other cattle, and bouncing off the fences. There was no way to cut this steer out of the pen, so as he came by, Joe roped him around the neck, and I roped one hind foot.

We kept the steer between us as we sawed him down to the hospital pen. We were able to keep him from getting too close to our horses or us, and once we had him in the crowding pen, we threw our ropes in with him. I spurred my horse and galloped to the office to call the state vet.

We knew it was rabies. The vet advised us to keep an eye on the steer and not make any direct contact with him. While I was in the office, the Okie car dealer called with his daily complaint. I told him to stop calling because his cattle were quarantined for rabies, and whoever he had bought them from was responsible. That shut him up. I promised I'd call him when the state vet had completed his evaluation.

The next day, the vet showed up, and that damn steer was acting as normal as could be—no symptoms at all. The vet drew some blood and said he'd call back. He didn't think the steer had rabies, but he couldn't tell us what was wrong.

The next day, the vet called again with no new answers, but the steer was still fine, so we put him in a pen with the other cattle. After two weeks, that steer was the fattest one in the pen—no sign of rabies. I ordered trucks and shipped the entire group of cattle to grass. Then, I called Mr. Okie car dealer to let him know they were gone.

I thought that would make him happy. Nope. Instead, I got my butt chewed for letting that steer get rabies!

Can't win.

Ropin' the Bulls

While at AZL, I had the chance to work with some good cowboys and ropers. One of my closest friends was Joe—a natural roper, horseman, and prankster. He came from a long line of cowboys and rodeo hands, with his dad having won the Prescott Rodeo several times.

At any feedlot, there are always a few bull calves that escape the knife due to sickness, lameness, or various other reasons. If things get busy, they might be forgotten for a month or two, and in that time, they get *big*.

At AZL, there was a crew we called the "vets." They weren't real veterinarians, but they drove around in pickups, doctored the sick cattle that cowboys found, and put them in a hospital pen with a squeeze chute for treatment. Once in a while, when things slowed down, they'd recruit a couple of us with itchy arms and ropes to help with the bulls. We'd rope the missed ones and stretch them out while the vets did their work.

One day, they got Joe and me to help put down half a dozen of these bulls. The first bull trotted by, and Joe flipped an overhand loop at him, catching him around the neck and figure-eighting the front feet. When the slack came tight, the bull dropped to his side with both front feet pulled up under his jaw. All I had to do was trot up and drop my loop over his hind feet. Once stretched out, the bull couldn't choke because his front feet acted as a block, keeping the rope from cutting off his airway. No fuss, no muss.

When the vet was finished, he laughed and said, "Too bad Joe can't do that every time!" Joe, ever the confident one, grinned and replied that he could—and would—for a case of beer. The vet, never one to back down from a challenge, called the bet.

After work that night, Joe and I had a cold beer at the boys' expense. And, true to form, Joe never let them forget it!

Eatin' is Just a Habit

My old friend Clayton had taken over the Arlington feedlot and needed some cowboys. I was out of work, with two kids, a wife, and a third on the way. The only thing keeping us from starvation was the winnings from a jackass ropin' contest. So, we moved to Arlington. It was a heck of a deal. We were given a four-bedroom frame house that had once been occupied by a bachelor cowboy. And I mean *campin'*—he had just a bed and barely anything else. He was supposed to leave in a month or so, just needing a room and three square meals, or so we were told. After half a day of cleaning out the trash and whatever else had piled up, we moved in and settled as best we could.

The next morning, I went to work with the bachelor and three other hands, one of whom was my old friend Pete. Pete had been there a few months longer than me and had been recruited by Clayton, same as I had been. Pete and I paired up and rode together, since we had worked together for six years at Taveras. Every once in a while, the bachelor would join us, but mostly, he was the floater, filling in on someone's day off.

When the first day ended and we all started home, the bachelor and I headed back to the house together. Pete had warned me that the bachelor was a weird duck, but he seemed fine to me—always joking around and clowning. When we got home, the Mrs. had cooked a hell of a supper: chicken-fried steak, potatoes, gravy, corn, and apple pie.

But when the bachelor came into the house, he sniffed the air, turned around, and went to his room. We waited a few minutes, thinking he was cleaning up or something. When he didn't return, I went to his door and knocked. He hollered, "Come on in!" There he was, sitting on his bedroll, eating a cheese sandwich.

I told him supper was waiting, but he just shook his head. "I can't eat that," he said. When I asked why, he replied that it smelled good, but he didn't believe in spending money on food that way. I told him he hadn't spent a penny on it, and that no one could eat cheese sandwiches while we were sitting down to a meal like that without at least giving it a try. But he still refused, saying, "Eatin' is just a habit, and you can break it if you try hard enough!"

Well, from then on, until he left, the Mrs. wouldn't speak to him. He ate his cheese sandwiches and rolled grain from the feed mill, which he'd pour milk and sugar on for cereal. I never knew if he managed to break the habit, but I sure wasn't going to try it myself!

AZL's Old Goat

When I worked for AZL in the early '70s, they bought a big cattle operation in Florida—the craziest cattle we ever saw. The joke around the place was that the gators made 'em crazy! After about six months, the higher-ups decided that the ranch needed an Arizona cow boss. Chas was given the duty. He was a good, young man with a lot of cow experience, but all out west. Still, he was up for the challenge. He recruited a handful of solid Arizona cowboys, many of whom thought they were better than the whip-crackin', web-toed cracker cowboys from Florida. One of them was Kenny.

Now, Kenny was a little rowdy... no, scratch that—he was a lot rowdy! The super at Hughes and Ganz, where I worked, was a guy in his mid-50s who had married a very attractive young woman, around 20. Well, everyone at the ranch teased him about being an old goat, chasing after that young girl and marrying her. Kenny made it clear that it was sinful and that he should repent so *he* could have her! That didn't sit well with the super.

Now, the super was a hell of a guy, especially for someone his age. You'd have to look pretty close to tell he was in his 40s. Me and this super were good friends. We roped together and socialized, and to be honest, this cute young thing he was married to was a problem. She had a bad attitude toward the hired hands and made life miserable for him. So when Chas recruited Kenny to go to Florida, the super breathed a sigh of relief. One less problem to deal with, and no more daily harassment about being an old goat.

When Chas and the crew got to Florida, they found the ranch stocked with red Brahman-cross cows that acted like deer, a good-sized herd of wild boars, and a small bunch of goats that had gone wild. Kenny called back a couple of times to give updates on how things were going. It didn't sound like much fun—sinkholes, gators, big snakes, and everything rotting from the moisture and humidity.

After about a month, Kenny called to say he was loading a truck for Hughes and Ganz, and on the truck was a present for the super. Two days later, I was unloading that truck. When the gate opened, a big red bull bolted down the chute, kicked at my horse as he went by, ran onto the scales, and then promptly jumped the back gate, continuing on his way! I asked the weigh master if he'd caught the weight, but he didn't see the humor. While the other cowboys tried to coax the red bull to join the party, I finished unloading the truck.

When the last animal was off, I led the cattle to the scales and closed the gate behind them. As I looked back, I saw the truck driver waving me over. I loped over, and he handed me an envelope addressed to the super. "Okay, now what?" I thought. Off the truck came the stinkiest old billy goat I'd ever seen. My horse liked the smell even less than I did and took off running, but I finally got him under control. I opened a pen and let the goat into it. I told the water trough washer to feed him some hay, then headed off to deliver the envelope to the super.

When the super opened the envelope, his face turned red, then white, and he started shaking. He stood up, looked out the window at that goat from Florida, looked at me, and said, "Get rid of him." "How?" I asked. "I don't care," he said, "turn him loose, eat him, I don't care!"

I never knew what Kenny had written in that note, but it took me a week to find someone willing to take that goat off my hands. I think he ended up in some tacos!

New Shirt

The stockyards complex in Phoenix was quite the operation—a sale barn, livestock supply store, office complex, bank, and the Stockman's Steak House! Next to the sale barn was a little greasy spoon café run by Buster's wife. So, twice a day, we cowboys would drop by the café to hang out. Breakfast was usually a fried egg sandwich, and lunch was either a special or a burger. After eating, we'd wander over to the livestock supply store, which was operated by a local team roper. We'd spend hours there, shooting the bull, inspecting bridle bits, and running our hands over new saddles. We always bought our ropes there—either work ropes or arena ropes. Back then, when you bought a new rope, it was pulled off a coil to the length you wanted, and you tied the knots, attached the honda, and sewed your own burner. Everyone knew how to do it.

One day, Buster had bought a ready-made rope—the first one I'd ever seen. Now, Buster was a big man—not particularly tall, but solid. Broad shoulders, deep chest, slim waist, and biceps that stretched the sleeves of his shirt to their limit. His hands looked like they were carved from a mesquite stump. He was known to have a short temper, though it wasn't as bad as it had been in his younger days. At the time, Buster was nearly 70.

Buster tied his new rope to the saddle horn, as was the custom, where it stayed until it wore out. The next morning, while doctoring some sick cattle, Buster noticed the new rope had stranded. This meant one of the three strands that made up the rope had broken. This was dangerous, as the remaining two strands now had to carry the full load of three.

Now, nylon ropes are great—until they break. They stretch an unbelievable amount, but once they snap, they act like a rubber band and can cause a lot of harm. Buster trotted to the saddle house, grabbed another rope, and threw the damaged one in the back of his truck.

At lunch, we were all talking about how a new rope could strand, and we agreed it must have been a flaw in the manufacturing process. After lunch, we all headed down to the livestock supply store. Buster brought the new rope with him. He gently laid it on the counter and explained to Tim, the store manager, what had happened and that he'd just take a refund or exchange it for a length off the coil.

Tim shook his head and told Buster he couldn't give a refund or exchange the rope because he thought it had been cut on a pipe post when Buster roped a steer. Buster assured Tim that wasn't the case and swore that Buster's story was true. Tim leaned forward into Buster's face and said, "You old son of a gun, you don't know what you want!"

Buster's hand shot out and grabbed Tim by the neck of his shirt. The back of Buster's neck was as red as a fire truck! I had a clear view of the whole thing. Buster's right fist was balled up, pulled back, and ready to deliver a day-ending punch to Tim.

Before anyone knew what happened, Tim was scrambling out the back door, and Buster was left holding a handful of rags—Tim's shirt, torn clean off.

Tim didn't come back for his shirt for a long time. I heard later that Taveras ended up paying for the shirt just to keep the peace in the neighborhood!

The Beginning

In the early '70s, I was feeling pretty unsettled. I had just gone through a divorce, and the job I loved was about to change. I didn't want to stick around, so I quit and spent a while drifting. What I really wanted was to hit the road in the summer, running up through Colorado, Wyoming, and Montana to rope. I didn't have a solid rope horse, but I figured I could make one in a few months, given the right circumstances.

I worked on a contract branding crew for a while and did some day work to fill in the gaps. Then I found a good palomino that didn't cost much and was started as a head horse. Now, I just needed a place to finish him off. That opportunity came calling one Sunday morning in the form of AZL.

By Monday, I had moved to Queen Creek, settled into a single-wide trailer, and stabled the palomino in the barn. Tuesday, I went to work. AZL had an arena, practice steers, and you could practice four days a week. Perfect. After a few weeks of practice, I felt old Rabbit was ready for a cheap jackpot roping or two.

Every Saturday night, there was a roping at 35th and Baseline at a place called Ike's. It became a regular hangout. I could rope a lot for not a lot of money, and usually, I made a little.

There was a young Mexican kid who hung out with me when I wasn't working. He never went home until he had to. He had a bunch of brothers and sisters, and he was the smallest in the litter. I started taking him with me when I roped somewhere. His dad was also a cowboy there, so naturally, Carlos wanted to rope too. It didn't take long to realize he was a natural.

One spring evening, Carlos and I were at Ike's. I was letting him warm up my horse while I fished around for partners. Parked at the fence was a '66 El Camino with a blanket on the hood, and on the blanket, there were two of the prettiest gals I had ever seen. By the end of the roping, I had a date to take them for coffee. The blonde jabbered like her jaw was unhinged, and the brunette— you couldn't pry a word out of her.

Carlos, my little traveling partner, wasn't happy with this deal at all. And as I found out later, the gals thought Carlos was my kid! But as time went on, we straightened everything out. I kept seeing that cute brunette, and soon, I started forgetting about that trip north.

By the end of the summer, that cute brunette and I were married. That began a life full of rodeos, ranches, feedlots, three kids, a lot of misery, but even more good times. I never regretted for a minute not going north. THAT was the beginning!!

Hughie

Hugh wasn't from Arizona. I'm not sure where he was from, but he was a good hand in the feedlots and the rodeo arena. The only time I actually worked with him was on a contract branding crew one winter, though I'd seen him around at feedlot ropings and jackpot ropings. He was likable, always sporting that big toothy smile.

Back in the early '70s, the guys who wanted to rodeo would often work on contract crews branding cattle in the feedlots around Arizona. You got paid by the head, and at a time when day wages were around $25, you could pull down a hundred or more a day. But you had to be on a crew willing to work hard, and that meant long hours if you wanted to make that kind of money.

On our crew, Hugh and I were the only ropers; the rest were bronc riders.

After a twenty-hour shift at a feed yard, we shut down to grab a hot meal and change clothes. Branding chute work at a feedlot is bloody, nasty work. We told the feedlot we'd be back in twelve hours to start again.

We dropped Hugh off at his little trailer, then scattered to head home for a shower, a meal, and a nap before meeting again in eight hours.

But when it was time to meet up, Hugh was nowhere to be found. We swung by his trailer to wake him up. When we pulled up, he was sitting on the front steps, wrapped up in his arms. This was midnight in January. Sure, Arizona winters aren't as cold as other places, but midnight in January still gets pretty chilly. Hugh was still wearing his dirty clothes, his hair sticking out from under his Resistol, and he wasn't smiling as usual.

He climbed into the truck, looking pretty miserable, and asked if we could stop at Jack in the Box. He was hungry. We grabbed some burgers and coffee at the drive-through. After he ate, he finally told us what had happened.

It turned out that when we dropped him off, he found his house occupied. His friend Donnie had brought a girl he'd picked up at the bar and was in Hugh's bed. They locked him out and wouldn't let him in. His truck keys were inside. Hugh said he begged and pleaded, but the two drunks just laughed at him. Finally, Hugh gave up and went for a walk. He tried to find somewhere to eat, but he was so nasty and smelled so bad, nobody would let him in.

When he finally came back to his place, he was freezing, starving, and exhausted. He was about to break a window to get in when we showed up. Poor guy was frozen, hungry, filthy, and tired.

We later found out that while he was walking around, Donnie and the girl had left. Hugh never tried the door when he got back. He told us the girl's perfume was so strong that it stained his blankets and wouldn't wash out. When Donnie sobered up, he apologized, but I don't think Hughie ever forgave him!

Sam and the Health Department

In the late '60s and early '70s, livestock pharmaceuticals were pretty primitive compared to today. I was workin' at the T&C Cattle Co. in Maricopa. We were processing and feeding out 25 thousand Mexican steers every 120 days. That was before it was unhealthy to eat meat, especially fat meat.

When we processed cattle then, we castrated bulls, branded, and maybe gave two vaccines. If the cattle had grubs, they got a cup of pour-on spilled on their backs. That was it! We shipped the fats to a Swift plant in Tolleson, Herseth Pack in Phoenix, Crockett Pack in Phoenix, Arizona Beef in Phoenix, and a dozen packing houses on Vernon Street in Los Angeles.

As the industry heated up, we began to hear about cattle with "measles." We never saw any cattle with red spots, but then we found out they were referring to carcasses with red spots. These red spots were tapeworm larvae embedded in the tissue of beef.

Back then, they were hand-trimmed out of the carcass, and later, frozen solid to kill them. Well, the packing house people were screaming their heads off at the feedlots, who screamed back. Then, the health department got involved. They decided employees at the feedlots were defecating in the feed troughs, and the cattle would eat the crap with tapeworm eggs, causing the cattle to get measles.

So, all the feedlots were to install outhouses out in the yards. Some called the porta-potty companies, others built them, and in the case of AZL, we built brick outhouses. Taveras were the worst measles offenders, which no one could figure out why. The fact that 90 percent of our cattle were straight out of Mexico was not considered.

Working in the yards was an old Mexican man named Serafin, and yes, I'm pretty sure he was illegal, but in those days, no one thought anything of it.

One day, Sam, the superintendent, called all the employees to the scale house. There, waiting for us, was a representative of the State Health Department. He gave us all a little speech about crapping in the feed trough and handed each of us a brown paper bag with a plastic sandwich bag inside. We were instructed to place a "specimen" in the sandwich bag, then place the plastic bag in the paper bag, label our names on the outside, and turn it into him the next day.

Well, Serafin spoke no English, and by the time it was translated to him, his eyes got that deer-in-the-headlights look! To the rest of us, this was the biggest joke in years. How far-fetched it got was a mystery to all of us, but we were told to go along with it or lose our jobs.

The next day, there were a dozen brown paper bags in a box on Sam's desk, all labeled, and some were decorated quite artistically. But Serafin's bag was absent. As a matter of fact, Serafin was absent. We went to look for him and found him washing water troughs out in the pens. When asked about his bag, he ignored the question. Sam was starting to get mad.

Serafin turned his back on us and said in Spanish that it was an unholy thing to do. Sam didn't want to lose Serafin, as he was dependable and a hard worker, but he couldn't avoid the problem. We put Serafin in the pickup and drove him to the scale house. Sam handed Serafin his bag, and he handed it back, shaking his head. Sam told him in Spanish to take the bag, fill it, or we would tie up a leg and collect the desired sample ourselves!

A few minutes later, the old man delivered the bag, head hanging.

Everyone was cleared—no tapeworms resided at our yard. Then they came up with cattle wormer that worked, and the problem went away, but Serafin was already gone, back to Mexico. He said all them damn gringos were unholy!

Clayton Drove Cadillacs

Clayton was a cowman of legend. He smoked big Havana cigars, wore the best clothes, talked loud no matter where he was, and was a first-rate cowman. He bought cattle for Taveras feedlots, managed some of the biggest ranches in Arizona, and knew every cowboy, rancher, cattle feeder, and truck driver by their first names. Always ready for a laugh—at your expense or his—it didn't matter. His wife, Delores, was one of the most beautiful women I've ever seen. When traveling the West buying cattle, she drove, and Clayton kept his books while talking on one of the first satellite phones I'd ever heard of. He was a high roller of the first order.

Once, when I was unloading trucks at night at the Maricopa yard, he called to tell me some instructions on a specific load of cattle. All at once, he went to hollering, "Watch out, watch out! Oooooh, look out!!!" When he settled down, I asked what the deal was. He said Delores was driving, and the California traffic had them surrounded like a bunch of piss ants!

After I left Taveras, I got married and traveled around working on ranches and at other feedlots. One day, I woke up with no job, a wife, two kids, and one on the way. Somehow, Clayton got word and tracked me down. He had taken over the management of a bankrupt feedyard for a bank and needed help. He already had my friend Pete there, so I went to Arlington. Clayton always had good horses—real good horses. When I moved in, I found I had my own horse corrals stocked with extra good two- and three-year-old colts, ready to start. I had plenty to do, and Clayton checked on me daily to see how his colts were doing and to make sure I wouldn't pull the picket pin and move on. He didn't know it, but I was staying as long as he would let me.

That summer, the dust in that feedyard was horrible. The cattle were getting sick from it, as were the employees who lived there. Clayton, somewhere, got a hold of an 8,000-gallon Euclid water pull, a big tank with a motor on it! Not many people knew how to run that thing, but they broke in a young Mexican boy who was settling the dust as fast as he could. Clayton had just bought a new Cadillac, as pretty a car as you could ever hope to see. He picked it up in Phoenix and drove straight to the yard, parking in front of the scale house. He was talking to Pete and me when around the corner came the Euclid.

The Mexican kid slowed down, then turned off the key in preparation to stop. One problem: when you turn off the key, everything ceases to work. No brakes, no steering, nothing! The tires on that thing were eight feet tall, and they just kept rolling… right over the top of that new Cadillac! It was smashed to about four feet tall, with black tire tread down the middle from trunk to hood. We looked at Clayton—his cigar was dangling at about six o'clock, and a fire was starting to ignite in his eyes! Pete looked at me and simply said, "Time to go." We left.

Clayton drove a pickup for a week or so until his special-order car came in. The Mexican kid disappeared, and all vehicles were ordered to park across the yard in a safe place!

Sam and the DEQ

The old T&C Cattle Co. feedlot lay along the highway between Maricopa and Casa Grande. When it was built, there was very little traffic on that road. The Southern Pacific rail line ran through there, as it had for a hundred years. It no longer stopped trains in Maricopa, but the water towers still stood when I was a kid. Maricopa was a junction in the old days, with a spur line running to the new farming community of Phoenix. Well, the spur line closed down, and the roadbed became Maricopa Road, a two-lane asphalt road when I was young. Today, it's a four-lane divided highway.

When I worked at the T&C, the Casa Grande highway was only traveled by farm folks going shopping in Casa Grande. There were some farmhouses in the vicinity, but the people who lived there were mostly cotton farmers. Well, that was the attitude we took. Never mind that I grew up in a cotton farming household. Hell, I worked for a cow outfit, so I was one of them. A fact of life around a feedlot was that, in the summer, when the sun went down and the air started to cool, those fat cattle would start bucking, bawling, and playing. Twenty-five thousand of those would raise quite a dust cloud, which was made up of manure, dried and powdered. To those of us used to it, we just smelled cash. To those with sensitive olfactory senses, it stunk!

Sam was the boss at T&C, no question about it. He was the boss. We all loved working for him because he let you cowboy. You weren't just a farmer on a horse, you were a cowboy. Sam had a temper, was cocky, and liked to play and joke—hard. He didn't put up with whining or complaining, but if you did your best, he gave you every break. Loyalty to the company was expected, and the company earned it.

Sam saw to it. Sam worked you hard, long hours, and sometimes you might think he took advantage of you, but somewhere down the road, he paid it back in triplicate.

One afternoon, we, the crew with Sam, had finished sorting some fat cattle and were lounging in the scale house, drinking soda pop and telling rodeo tales. I was too young to tell any, but I ate up the ones Sam, A.O., and Gilbert told. They had known Buckshot Sorrels, Hugh Bennit, and untold others who were legendary. We were aware of some of the neighbors complaining about the dust in the evening, but we had a sprinkler system that kinda worked. Besides, we didn't tolerate whiners. While sitting there slurping soda, a white sedan with state government plates pulled up outside, and a gray-haired fella in a black suit got out. He walked into the scale house, looked around, nodded, and turned to Sam, who was behind the desk.

"Do you know where I could find Ed Tavera, Harold Christopherson, or Sam White?" he asked.

Sam grinned and said, "I don't know, do you have warrants for them?"

The old man said, "I very well may have!"

Sam stood up, put his feet on the floor, and asked who the old man was. The fellow produced a badge and a set of papers. At that, the rest of us made a retreat out the back door!

As it turned out, he was from the State Department of Environmental Quality. He was there to put a stop to the dust that rose out of that feedlot every night. Well, the bottom line was the company bought two water trucks and rigged them to spray into the pens as they were driving along. It took a good month before the dust settled enough to see a difference. We cowboys often had to drive those trucks—something we sure didn't like— but Sam said do it, so we did.

A.D. Lost His Thumb

When I worked at Taveras, there was a cowboy I kind of looked up to. He was as good a cowboy and horseman as you could ask for. He'd trained racehorses, rodeoed, ran ranches, and lived a wild, raucous life. Trouble was, that wild raucous life was mostly illegal!!

His name was A.O. He liked to tell people it stood for "After Death!" He drank whiskey like water, dipped Copenhagen snuff, cussed a blue streak, and was generally a pain in the butt, but he was a cowboy. He was prematurely gray-headed, about six feet tall, and lean as a whip. Tom T. Hall's song *Faster Horses* could have been written about A.O.; if it wasn't, it should've been! A.O. was a team roper, a damn good one—header or heeler, it didn't matter. I saw him rope for weeks without missing a loop. His horses were fast, quick, and deadly. They had to be because his temper was a terrible thing to behold— man or beast!

A.O.'s pride and joy was a sorrel, bald-faced, stocking-legged gelding named, you guessed it, *Socks!* When heading in the arena, Socks could run a hole in the wind and get you to a steer so fast, you couldn't get your loop up quick enough. The minute you turned that loop loose, he'd slide his left hind foot and run on the other three feet, turning that steer almost as fast as he was running forward. He was still a young horse, basically still learning, but he made that turn at full speed on his own. If the loop was to miss, there was no way to bring him back in line with the steer.

We were practicing one afternoon when A.O. roped a big steer. As he was dallying, Socks went left, and this time A.O.'s thumb got caught in the rope. With Socks' speed and the weight of the steer, that thumb came off like a knife had cut it off.

Sam's pickup was parked close, so we loaded A.O. in the middle and headed to the hospital, 18 miles away. As we passed Sam's house, he stopped, ran in, and returned with a bag of ice and a pint of whiskey. We wrapped A.O.'s hand in a towel and packed the ice around the mangled thumb. As we drove out the gate, Sam handed A.O. the whiskey and asked if he needed some. He was white as a sheet and shook his head no. That was the only time I ever saw him turn down a drink! But by the time we reached the hospital, A.O. had taken a healthy pull from that jug! Sam just said he didn't think A.O. was that bad off.

Sasabee

On the Mexican border, southwest of Tucson, lies the small village of Sasabee. The only commerce there comes from the ranches on either side of the border, making it a remote place for both Mexicans and Americans alike. On the Mexican side, one of the ranches belongs to the Osuna family. For generations, they've ranched there and worked on the American side for added income.

One of the Osuna family, Pablo, was a good friend of mine. Though he worked at a different feedlot than I did, we roped together at various ropings and spent time socializing. He had a large family and was always scrapping together side deals to keep the many mouths fed. I was also told that he helped support his brother, who lived at the ranch in Mexico. Pablo always rode the best-trained horses, even if they weren't the best-looking. I once saw a mule he trained that handled like a horse— could spin, slide, and work cattle like no other. When asked where he got it, Pablo simply smiled and pointed south. He'd often come up with really nice young horses, breaking them in and then selling them for a good price. I remember one palomino mare—about 14 hands and 1,000 pounds. She was quick as a cat and could run like the wind for about 150 yards. Pablo roped on her and cut cattle with her. She was a real gem. I asked him again one day where he got her. Once again, he smiled and pointed south.

About a month later, he asked me to drive him to Sasabee to visit his brother and wondered if I could pull his trailer. Sure, why not. When we were about a mile from Sasabee, Pablo had me turn off onto a two-track trail that ran alongside the international fence. About two miles into the trip, the road ended at a large mesquite thicket. Pablo jumped out, squatted down, and pointed into the thicket. There, I could see three sets of horse legs. Pablo whistled, and a young Mexican boy riding one horse bareback with two others in tow, came up to the truck. Pablo explained that the boy was his nephew, and that the horses were from the family ranch across the line. I asked how they'd gotten here. He smiled and told me to follow him.

The nephew rode his pony back into the thicket, and we followed. In the middle of the thicket was a hole sloping downward into the ground. The entrance was paved with concrete, and as we walked down the ramp, it became clear that it was a tunnel built to accommodate a truck. Pablo explained that, during prohibition, whiskey smugglers had built it to run whiskey into Tucson. When prohibition ended, the tunnel was forgotten, but the Osuna family kept using it as their own port of entry, taking horses and cattle back and forth through the tunnel.

I saw Pablo a few years ago and asked, with all the activity along that part of the border, if they still used the old tunnel. He shook his head sadly and said, "No, the Border Patrol found it and blew it up." "No más," he added, shaking his head.

Ed McFarkle

When I got to AZL, there was a heck of a crew already working there. Only a couple were cowboys, the rest were wannabes. Bud and Dude were real top hands. Jerry was my age and as single as I was, and we rode together—he was a good hand. Then there was Ed.

Ed was in his sixties, a heavy smoker and drinker. He had been a top rodeo hand in the '40s and '50s. He wasn't very big—maybe 5'4"—and if he weighed 110 pounds, I'll eat my hat. He had been a racehorse trainer in the Northwest. His health wouldn't let him stay in that wet country, so he came back to Arizona to get his lungs dried out, except those unfiltered cigarettes were wreaking havoc on him.

I don't know if he had ever been married—he didn't say. He still liked to rope and was after someone every week to go rope with him at a jackpot. The problem was, he was drunk before the roping was over, and if you were in his truck, he wouldn't let you drive. I only went with him one time like that—that was enough! He would be driving along, sucking on a beer, smoking a cigarette, and get to coughing. When that happened, there was no telling where his little truck would go! How we got back without getting killed, I'll never know. Because of that hacking cough, everyone started calling him McFarkle. He drove a Datsun pickup with a two-horse trailer. His rope horse, called Leo, was a trailer fighter. I wonder why. When Ed got to hacking, almost immediately, Leo would start scrambling in the trailer with Ed saying, "Wa wa wa, stand up Leo!"

We had been to a roping one night and started home when Ed decided we needed to stop at a bar on South Mountain. You had to drive up a steep driveway to get to the bar. We started up that grade, pulling two horses with a Datsun pickup with a four-cylinder motor! After downshifting three times, we stalled about a third of the way up. We started rolling backward slowly, with Ed hacking, Leo scrambling, and me trying to figure out how I would explain my presence in a hospital to my new boss and my folks! But thanks to the drunk gods, we coasted into an empty parking lot, jackknifing the trailer to a stop. Ed sat there in a stupor and finally looked up and said he needed a new truck because this one wouldn't get him to the bar! I was about ready to unload my horse and ride home! But Ed was done for the night, so I got to drive. That was never going to happen again! From then on, if Ed wanted to go, he went in my truck with me driving!

Then he bought a new full-size Dodge pickup. When behind the wheel, you just saw Ed's hat. He got stopped a few times for that! Ed left there the next year, and we never knew where he ended up, but he left a legacy that went on for a while!!

Tail Gates Are Dangerous

Over the years, I've seen tailgate accidents happen more times than I care to count, with results ranging from a scratch to unconsciousness and stitches.

I was working in the Tavera yard in Phoenix. One of the principals there raised registered Charolais cattle on the side. One Saturday afternoon, I was the only one at the yard, just putting in my time. A kid named Billy, whose father was a feed truck driver, was hanging around waiting for his dad to get off work. Harold, the owner of the registered cattle, called the scale house and asked if I would take the company pickup and trailer to the sale yard to pick up a bull that had been mistakenly left behind. Since I didn't have much else to do, I agreed to the chore. Billy wanted to come along, and I didn't see any harm in it—we'd only be gone a few minutes.

The truck was a Chevy short-bed pickup, and the trailer was a bumper-pull Hale stock trailer with wooden slats bolted in place.

When we got to the sale barn, there wasn't a soul to be found. We parked the trailer and started looking for the bull. After a few minutes, we found him—a big bull locked in a dry corral, about as big as a postage stamp. He'd been there for a couple of days, with no water or feed. When I opened the gate, the bull came at us like a locomotive, head down, thundering by. I quickly stepped behind the gatepost, and as the bull charged up the alley, I jogged along behind him.

Billy was sitting on the fence by the trailer, out of harm's way. As we got close to the trailer, I yelled at the bull, who broke into a run with me hot on his heels. As the bull jumped into the trailer, I swung the tailgate shut—just as the bull switched ends inside the trailer. Then, everything went dark.

When I came to, I was sitting on the ground at the end of the trailer. The bull was still inside, the gate was latched, and Billy was washing my face with a wet rag. My head felt like a trip hammer was going off inside it.

Billy said the bull had hit the end gate just as I was shutting it, and the gate struck me in the forehead. He said I latched the gate and then just sat down. I had a three-inch gash in my forehead where one of the bolts in the tailgate had hit me square between the eyes. The wet rag Billy was using to bathe my face was soaked with blood.

After unloading the bull and heading back home, Billy's dad drove me to the emergency room, where I got a tetanus shot and five stitches in my head. I took aspirin for a week before that trip hammer feeling finally stopped.

I was lucky. I've known truckers loading fat cattle who've had their teeth knocked out, jaws broken, or even lost an eye. I saw a horseshoer get slammed in the face by a kicked tailgate while helping load a bronc. So, folks, watch those tailgates. They are dangerous!

Promotion

When President Nixon was in office, he and his economic team decided that the U.S. industry needed to stop giving raises and perks, believing it would help the economy. That idea didn't last long, but it came at a time when feedlot cowboys were struggling financially and needed every dime we could earn.

When the freeze was put into effect, a bunch of us at Toveras were pretty upset. We hadn't had a raise in two years, and the cost of living was creeping up daily. Besides, entry fees at rodeos and jackpots were going up!

The owners sent word down through Sam that there would be no raises. I remember Sam turning red in the face, his hands shaking, and his temper taking control for a brief moment. We all wanted to be somewhere else, real quick, but Sam wasn't having any of it. He grabbed the phone, and within seconds, he had Mr. Tavera on the line. He reminded him of our loyalty and how we had been promised raises. Sam listened for about a half-minute or so, his face getting redder, then, in a quiet but firm and stern voice, he said, "If I lose one man over this, I'm going with him." Then he hung up the phone and looked at all of us. "I don't blame any of you if you walk out," he said. Before he finished speaking, the phone rang again. Sam answered, listened for a second, said goodbye, and hung up. "The bookkeeper will be here tomorrow, boys. Will you hang on until then?" We all agreed to wait until the bookkeeper arrived. I don't think any of us had actually planned to leave, but no one vocalized it.

The next day, when the bookkeeper arrived, Sam called us all into the scale house to hear what he had to say. The bookkeeper had studied the ruling and found a loophole: if you were promoted to a more responsible position, you could receive a raise. So, Gilbert was promoted from pen rider to head of the shipping department. Pete was promoted from pen rider to head of the processing department. I was promoted from barn manager (colt breaker) to pen rider. And AD was promoted to water truck manager. In this way, we all got a $50-a-month raise!

Now, this was all on paper, because none of us actually changed what we had been doing for four years.

You know the sad part? I don't think Sam got a raise, but he was ready to go to bat for the rest of us!

Colts

When I graduated high school, I had no interest in spending my summer working on the cotton farm my dad ran. After a long stretch of hoeing weeds, irrigating cotton, and doing other miserable jobs, I felt like that kind of work was meant for lower-class folks. But there wasn't much else to do in my hometown at the time—cotton was the main industry. There were a few feedlots in town, but the chances of getting a job there seemed slim to none.

Or so I thought.

One evening, the phone rang, and my dad answered it. After hanging up, he let us in on what was going on. Back in those days, you didn't eavesdrop on a phone call—at least not in our house, not if you knew what was good for you.

It turned out the manager at Toveras—also known as T&C Cattle Company—needed someone to start colts. If it worked out, I'd have a part-time job in the fall when I went back to school. My dad had told Sam he could get by without me, seeing as I wasn't exactly cut out for cotton farming.

Sam and my dad went to church together, and Sam had seen some of the colts I'd started in high school. He thought I might be the right fit. So, I showed up to work with a Porter's saddle, a hackamore, and the kind of know-it-all attitude that only a young man with little experience can have. Little did I know, I was about to get a crash course in horsemanship.

Sam White knew more ways to gentle a colt and put a finish on one than anyone I'd ever met. Many top-notch horse trainers started out working for Sam before moving on to bigger things. I can't say I followed in their footsteps, but I did have some success with the horses I worked with. Over the years, I showed horses, including the state champion stallion for two years in a row, and qualified him for the national show in all the cattle events—thanks to everything I learned from Sam.

Sam would often sit by the round corral while I worked with a green colt, talking to me as I went. Without realizing it, I was learning from him all the time, picking up techniques that would stay with me.

I also discovered that Sam had a bit of a prankster side—though a rough one. I'd spend a week in the round pen with a colt, getting in a ride or two, then would slip them outside. There wasn't much open country around, just an asphalt road leading to the main gate of the feedlot. The scale house, with its big windows, overlooked the road and the horse barn.

One of the first colts I took out was skittish and temperamental. We'd already had a runaway in the round pen, but I thought he was ready for the road. As I got close to the gate, I looked up and saw Sam rolling a metal garbage can straight toward us! The colt froze for a split second, then took off like a bullet. I went along for the ride, trying to hang on. It took me another week to get that colt back to the gate, every time he would snort, stamp his foot, and if he couldn't run off, he'd back up! Meanwhile, Sam was laughing himself silly.

I got my revenge, though.

One morning, we were weighing fat cattle. The last five steers refused to take the last step onto the scales, and two of us were horseback, pushing the gate as hard as we could, hollering and cussing. Sam came out of the scale house with a hot shot in hand, handing me the handle while he held the business end. When I grabbed the handle, I accidentally hit the button. Sam let out a yell, and I quickly apologized. After a moment, he smiled and said, "We're even."

Over the next six years, I started all the colts at Toveras, except for one crop of horses while I was in the service. And what a crop they were. Two full brothers, Rebel Cause and Tonto Bar Gill, both went to the track and could run like the wind. The oldest won the consolation race at the All-American. Some of the horses were foundation-bred Quarter Horses—Buzzy Bell H, Tony, Music Mount, Pelican, and Hancock. The mares were bred to Rebel Cause, Vanguard, Little Request, and a little Leo-Yellow Wolf stud from New Mexico. He was just a cow pony stud, but I think his colts were the best of the bunch.

When I found out by accident that Sam was leaving, I didn't see any sense in sticking around. Since then, I've never encountered another cow outfit, feedlot, or ranch with horses quite like the ones Sam bred. Of course, it's easy to look back and say they were the best, but I'll always believe they were.

The Great Potato Stampede

While I was working at Hughes and Ganz, a division of AZL, we had a couple of large pens about a half mile from the main yard, behind the hay barns. These were called the pasture pens, and together they could hold nearly a thousand steers. We never put anything down there that wasn't at least half-finished because it was a hassle to doctor fresh cattle there. Half-finished cattle were generally less prone to sickness and caused fewer problems, unless you count the trouble of moving them from the main yard.

There was no dedicated lane from the main yard to those pens. The gate that allowed access was a small ten-footer, right in the middle of a fence—a tricky spot for moving cattle through.

The road leading to the pens was a narrow, one-lane affair, elevated between two irrigated potato fields. Word came down that we were going to send a fresh batch of cattle to the pasture pens. It would take a combined crew from sections one and two—twelve men. You'd think that would be enough, but it wasn't. The section boss from section two was supposed to empty the pens at the main yard and send the cattle down an alley to us, waiting outside. The smart thing would've been to move them in one- or two-hundred head lots, but no—Jack kicked the whole thousand out to us.

The cattle got to bucking, bawling, and playing on the dry, powdery ground until the dust was so thick you couldn't see your hand in front of your face. The section boss from section one came by at a lope and told me he'd take the lead down that little narrow road to the pens. My job was to turn the thousand half-fat, crossbred steers down the ten-foot-wide road with irrigated potatoes on both sides. The rest of the boys were doing everything they could to keep the herd in one pile, but that was no easy task.

Then Jack showed up, hollering, and rode straight through the middle of the herd at a trot. His plan was to get some of the leaders onto the road so the rest would follow. But with all that dust flying, nobody saw those handful of steers break off and take the road. Jack never looked back, just kept hollering and running those steers up the road.

Two of the cowboys on the potato patch side saw what was happening and spread the word to shove the cattle to the road all at once. I managed to turn the leaders, and the herd took the road. But with that many cattle, they couldn't all fit. On each side of the road, the steers spilled out into the fresh irrigated potatoes, tromping them into a muddy mess! We tried to get them back on the road but bogged our horses down to the saddle skirts. That bunch of steers churned up the potato patches and then turned back toward home.

We held them off for a bit, but before we could stop them, they stampeded into the potatoes again. With the damage done, we charged the steers toward that tiny ten-foot gate and the two men waiting to turn them in. Some made it through, but most didn't and went past. We had to round them up on dry ground and hold them until they calmed down. By now, it wasn't too hard—those steers were exhausted. Once they settled, they strung out in a line like cattle should, walked to the gate, and entered as calm as could be.

We knew AZL had to pay for the potato crop, but we never heard how much. Potato chip potatoes didn't come cheap even then. After that day, any time cattle were moved to or from the pasture pens, it was done only when the fields were dry and in 100-head bunches. Jack ended up as a pickup driver, and I got his job.

Arizona's Cowtown

In the early 1960s, most of Arizona's commercial feedlots were concentrated in the Salt River Valley. They lined 48th Street in Phoenix, starting at Washington and extending south into the dry Salt River bed. However, a combination of a heavy winter, a hundred-year flood, and the housing boom wiped them out—some never reopened, while others relocated to different parts of the state.

Farmers in my hometown realized they could sell land to feedlot operators for new feeding grounds and grow the feed staples for fattening cattle. Feedlot owners, looking to relocate, wanted assurance that newcomers wouldn't sue to push them out. So, farmers, along with the feedlot owners, went to the state legislature and requested special zoning for a township dedicated to feedlots and packing houses. The request was granted, and construction began on the first feedlot, T&C Cattle Co., an extension of the Tavera family.

Soon, Smith and Kelly, followed by Producers, set up shop. At the far end of the township, John Wayne and Lewis Johnson built the renowned Red River Feed Lot. Cudahy bought land to build a new packing house between Smith and Kelly and T&C. Things were progressing well until the farmers got greedy, raising the land prices so high that other cattle feeders turned their backs and bought land elsewhere. McElhany built their feedlot in Wellton, Hughes and Ganz in Queen Creek, Spur Feeding on an Indian lease at Santan, Olen Dryer in Laveen, and Goodyear followed suit.

When the cotton growers realized they wouldn't be able to sell land to feedlot owners anymore, they pushed for the zoning to be changed. I was working at T&C when the state legislature's tour bus came through the feed yards. After visiting each lot and evaluating the situation, they adjourned to deliberate.

The cotton farmers were sure they'd win, but after a couple of weeks, the committee ruled that the cow town township would remain intact for 100 years. The farmers and developers were told that the zoning had been their request in the first place, and they had to live with it. They could still sell their land for homes, but the buyers had to sign an agreement acknowledging the presence of the feedlots. To my knowledge, the situation remains unchanged. While there are houses in the area, no attempts have been made to push out the cattle feeders.

I Don't Hire ###$$@@##$ Team Ropers!!!!

I've always roped. Wherever I worked, roping came first, but the job always came first. If it came down to a good job or going to a ropin', I stayed and worked. If the job was bad, well, that was a whole different kettle of fish.

In those years, I worked for Taveras and AZL, and they spoiled me. They provided arenas and cattle for their employees, supporting anyone who competed under the company name. While working for AZL, I qualified for the World Feedlot Championships twice. We saved our vacation time for the finals, and the company would chip in some financial support. They liked bragging about our success.

But not all feeders shared the same attitude. The ones who had the worst-managed yards and the least competent help were the most critical. They didn't pay well and complained constantly. They'd cheat their horses on feed or, in some cases, not have any horses at all. When they did have horses, they were usually cheap and unproductive.

I had a fair job with good people, a comfortable house, and some security, but I'd gone as far as I could go. The higher-tier jobs weren't available to hired help, mainly due to family concerns. One day, I learned that a local cattle feeder had fired his yard manager. I knew the fired manager—he knew the business but was prone to partying, drinking, and running around on his wife. He roped, but his personal habits kept him from winning much.

I called the feeder and expressed my interest in the job. He agreed to meet me the next day at his office. I showed up, dressed in my best cowboy attire, with a couple of letters of recommendation in hand. When I walked in, the man looked at the gold buckle on my belt, turned red, and began shaking.

"Get out!" he yelled. I was stunned. Before I could speak, he launched into a tirade. "You goddamn team ropers. All you do is get drunk, beat your horses, and cheat on your wives! Get out now!"

I left, deflated and disappointed. That night, Clayton, one of the men who'd written a letter for me, called to check in. I told him what had happened. He listened quietly, then said he thought the fired manager's antics might have ruined the deal for me.

Clayton assured me that even though the job paid more, I wouldn't have been happy for long. There was a reason the other guy drank and caused trouble. Over time, I saw many cattle feeders change yard bosses—most of them quit. Maybe that gold buckle saved me from a hard lesson.

Dude, Bugs, and the Ferrari

While I was at AZL, the super caught a wild bug and decided to buy himself a Ferrari sports car: fire-engine red, six inches off the ground, and 0 to 60 in 6.3 seconds. Just what you need to cruise around a feedlot. He had a carport built at the office specifically for the little Italian beauty. Every day, he'd drive the Ferrari to work, park it, and then use a company pickup to show fat cattle to buyers.

To the north of the office was the horse barn and saddle house, paved with asphalt all the way to the office. To the right was the feedlot, with gravel feed alleys and cattle pens. So the ride from the saddle house to the feedlot could get a little dicey, with slick surfaces, feedlot trucks, hay trucks, and all kinds of vehicles cruising around. Not the ideal place for gentle horses, much less colts and broncs.

Dude was one of the cowboys when I started working there. After a couple of years, the company changed policy, allowing cowboys to keep more than one personal mount. We all had our rope horses, but this new policy let us ride colts for others for pay, or buy a colt, train it, and sell it for extra income. Dude went to our old friend, Jack Clem, and bought a little stag bronc. This horse had run as a stud until he was eight years old, untouched by human hands before castration. He was as wild-eyed as you could imagine.

Dude kept this little hellion in a small, solid-walled pen with no chance of escape. He named him "BUGS" because of the horse's bug-eyed look. After a couple of weeks of hard work, Dude moved Bugs to the horse barn with the rest of the horses. Bugs didn't buck much, but he was unpredictable. Sometimes he'd try to run away; other times, he'd sulk and refuse to move at all.

When shipping fat cattle, we always saddled our broke horses. Afterward, we'd go to the saddle house for coffee and change into our green colts to ride pens. One morning, after coffee, Dude decided to saddle Bugs for a stint at checking pens. Bugs seemed docile as Dude saddled him. He had hobbled Bugs in front of the saddle house, and the horse stood as still as a statue while Dude cinched the saddle. But the calm was short-lived.

When Dude turned to grab his hackamore, Bugs farted, snorted, and suddenly wheeled on his hind feet. The little bay took off bucking across the pavement toward the office. The hobbles weren't slowing him down at all. Dude broke into a run, knowing he couldn't catch the horse before he reached the office, but he didn't know what else to do.

The Ferrari was parked in its usual spot in the carport, and Bugs was locked onto it like a heat-seeking missile! I could hear Dude muttering, "Oh shit, oh shit," as he ran after his horse. As Bugs approached the carport, he was in mid-air, bawling like a bull buffalo caught in a locomotive cowcatcher. At the peak of his jump, the saddle horn caught the lip of the roof, rattling the carport and jerking Bugs to the ground right behind the sports car. Before Bugs could regain his feet, Dude landed on him like a hen on a clutch of eggs!

I caught up on horseback, and Dude handed me the lead rope as he let Bugs up. The little horse kept trying to buck, but the lead was snubbed to my saddle horn, so he couldn't get unwound. We were trying to quietly slip away from the office when the front door opened. Dude ducked his head, knowing exactly what was coming.

Mr. Super stepped out slowly, not saying a word. He walked around the car, inspecting it carefully. When he reached the front fender and saw there was no damage, he turned to Dude and asked if Dude was planning to sell Bugs. Dude assured him he would. Mr. Super simply nodded and walked back into the office, shutting the door behind him. Dude wilted in relief. I thought he was going to pass out.

Sure enough, Dude sold Bugs three months later and made a handsome profit. But by then, Bugs was still unshod—and never allowed anywhere near red sports cars!

Colt Starter

While working for T&C Cattle Co., it was my job to start the colts each fall that the company had raised for the cowboys to use in the feed yard. After about 60 days, each cowboy would take one to add to their string. Feed yard work is tough on horses, and the lameness factor is high. There were always three or four broke horses turned out for one reason or another, so every horse was needed in turn.

A lot of funny things happened while I was starting colts. One day, a feller showed up looking for work. We were shorthanded, so Sam put him on and told him to be there the next morning at 5 a.m. The new hand showed up at 6—a little late, not a good sign. Sam was death on being late when it came to shipping fat cattle. He showed the new guy his horses, told him to shake a leg, jumped in his truck, and rushed back to the scale house. Meanwhile, I was in the round pen with a colt.

Now, this round pen was made out of railroad ties stood on end, side by side. There was a little crack between the ties, but other than that, it was a solid wall. Pretty soon, I heard someone clear his throat. Looking around, I couldn't see anyone. Again, the sound came, and I realized someone was peeking through the crack between two ties. I walked over, and the new guy asked me for help. I thought he had a serious problem, so I left my colt and followed him to the barn.

On the ground was a new Sears and Roebuck saddle with a cotton blanket, and a cheap import bit on a cardboard headstall lay in the dirt next to it. I asked him what the problem was, and he pointed to the rig on the ground, asking if I could show him how to use it. I almost passed out. I had heard him bragging to Sam about being some kind of 'whampus kitty' cowpuncher. I looked around to see who was watching, then, as quickly as I could, saddled his horse and made a hasty retreat to the round pen. This clown never untacked his horse—just crawled on and wallowed him around before ambling toward the scale house.

I stayed busy in the corral for most of the morning and was taking a breather, squatting next to the fence in the shade when someone above me told me I wasn't getting much done sitting there. I looked up, and Sam was grinning at me from on top of his horse.

I straightened up, pointed to the colt in the middle of the pen, dripping with sweat, and told Sam that he was on strike.

Sam sat there for a moment, then looked me in the eye and asked if I'd saddled the gunsel's horse. I told him I had. He asked why I hadn't said anything to him about it. I replied, "In the first place, I hadn't seen anyone until now, and secondly, I figured he'd figure it out."

Sam laughed and said I was right. Then he asked if I could go turn the horses out that he'd assigned the clown. The guy had already left.

It didn't take long with Sam. Try your best, tell him the truth, and he'd help you all day long. Lie to him or be lazy, though, and you'd be down the road.

Chasin' Ole Crooked Horn

When I worked for Taveras, they had pastured some steers with an outfit that had irrigated pasture next to the Gila River Indian Reservation. The Gila River passes through the middle of that land, and growing along its banks for miles is a patch of mesquite forest called the New York Thicket. It is one of the largest, continuous mesquite thickets in Arizona, maybe even the Southwest.

The river is usually dry, but in protected places, water comes to the surface for short distances. When Taveras shipped off the irrigated pasture, they found they were short about 50 head. These had ended up in the thicket. There were already an untold number of escapee cattle there, not to mention hundreds of wild horses. Taveras put a $50 bounty on the steers they were missing, so when we got a day off, some of us went to the river to try to earn a little reward money.

This one particular Sunday afternoon, the old-timer and I were prowling in the thicket. The tracks were thick, and the cow sign was everywhere. We started tracking a bunch of cattle downriver, and as we entered a clearing, we could see a little dust hanging in the air, maybe catch the smell of cow. We were that close. In the trail's powdery dust, there was one track that looked like a ski—long, narrow, and it belonged to a big animal. As the day went on, we kept after this bunch, hoping they would wear out. They never did.

By dark, we were six miles from our truck, with a long, dry ride back. The next morning at the feedlot, we weighed up the fat cattle to ship and were waiting for the brand inspector. His truck turned into the yard, pulling an open-top, bumper-pull stock trailer. Inside, standing a foot above the sideboards, were two of the biggest steers I'd ever seen. One was a Hereford, his head tied down to the floorboard to keep him from jumping out. Next to him, standing another foot taller than the Hereford, was a crossbred Mexican steer. He had a four-foot horn on one side, and the horn on the other had been broken and turned down, growing under the steer's neck and up to a point that almost touched the good horn on the other side!

The old-timer was looking around when something struck him, and he looked at the steer's feet. Sure enough, that long-toed track belonged to Ole Crooked Horn. When asked how they came by these steers, the Indian brand inspector explained that a couple of white cowboys had run them all day Sunday. When the moon came out, he and another Indian cowboy had caught the cattle on an alkali flat! Ole Crooked Horn had gored and killed one horse and hadn't given up easily.

They took those steers to the old Paramount Packing House in Casa Grande, and that Old Crooked Horn steer lived out his life there as a curiosity. The only brand that could still be read on him was last used in 1948—the year of my birth! That made that old steer 21 years old when he was caught. As Maxwell Smart would say, "Missed him by that much!"

RANCHES

Florence

Years ago, I was helping Dave down at Alamo Lake. We spent a lot of time in camp. One night, just at dark, Joe Beeler and some other folks showed up for supper. Among them was Joe's daughter, just back from Italy and studying art there. When Dave asked what she was up to, she explained that the school wanted to send her to Florence for more studying.

Dave said, "Hell, that ain't nothin'. Arizona's been tryin' to send me to Florence for years!"

Bob 'Shoefly' Shufelt

The last time I saw Bob "Shoefly" Shufelt, the great cowboy artist, was years ago at a brandin' in Aguila, Arizona. We had been working all day flankin' calves together. It was hot, dusty, and dry. We were sitting' on an old, dry water trough takin' a break when one of the punchers, who wasn't much of a hand, started braggin' about Texas. Bob unloaded on him:
"I'll tell you about Texas. Little pastures of a thousand acres, corrals built of pipe, and big ole hosses tied to a fence while they work their cattle through a calf table! These Arizona cowboys gather twenty sections, put the cattle in a net wire corral, and drag calves to the fire on the same thousand-pound horses they gathered on all day! Don't tell me about Texas!"

Mrs. Jefe and the Bankers

Years ago, Mrs. Jefe and I were gathering a bunch of steers to ship at the Ox Ranch. This particular day, the bankers were along. By 10 o'clock, it was HOT! Now, we never carried water, but these bankers kept whining about being thirsty. We had about 200 steers in the drive and were headed out of the pasture to the corrals. Every time the bankers asked about water, we just told them it was over the next ridge.

Mrs. Jefe was in the lead. When a windmill came in sight, the bankers were on the drags. The steers all lined up at the water trough with Mrs. Jefe at the top end. From where we sat, the bankers thought she was drinkin' out of the trough with the steers. They weren't very thirsty then. Actually, she was drinkin' from the pipe at the mill!

Someone's Prowlin'

Every year during round-up, Mrs. Jefe ALWAYS cooked chicken-fried steak—big meal, gravy, corn, biscuits, the whole works. We had a friend staying' with us. About 1 a.m., Mrs. Jefe woke me up.

"Someone's prowlin' the house," she says!
I tip-toed down the hall, and there, in the kitchen, was my friend in his underwear cutting a piece of steak.

"Just one more chunk," he said!!

Crossin' the Gila River Reservation

Years ago, when I was just a button, when school would let out for the summer, I'd saddle my pony at daylight and head to Chandler to stay at my grandparents' house. It was a 30-mile ride, but in them days, we didn't think much of it. One time, as I was crossing' the Gila River Indian Reservation, I ran into an Indian cowboy on my way. We rode together for a while. Pretty soon, we came across the old Snake Town site, a Hohokam site on the Gila River. The ground was a mosaic of broken pottery. My companion stopped his horse and looked around.

"My family maybe live here," he said. "Ole lady get mad at the ole man and break it ALL the dishes!!!"

With that, he turned his horse and rode off chucklin'!

Mr. Rose

Mr. Rose was an old-time rancher who, up in his 80s, was leasing' his ranch out, putting' in his time. To say he was a little eccentric would be kind. He still drove and got around but was kinda reckless. I had his ranch leased with a bunch of steers on it, but we didn't live there. Our home was on the highway to Wickenburg.

One day, when I got home, Mr. Rose's Cadillac was in the driveway. He was slumped over the wheel. Crap. I thought he cashed in. The front of the car was wrapped in barbed wire, and mesquite and greasewood were stuck in the grill.

I unloaded my horses and looked up—he was watching' me through the windshield. When I walked over to him, he smiled and asked if I could drive him

home. The Caddy had a hole in the radiator, and the engine was seized. Seemed he went to town for groceries, and on the way back, he went to sleep, ran off the road, woke up, tromped on the gas pedal, and shot back onto the road at a different place in the fence!!
That little deal cost a pretty penny, but he didn't seem to mind or quit driving'!

Hide and Seek

We were gathering the west pasture for the spring works. This was one of those times the owner and his wife wanted to ride along. The pasture was big, rough, brushy, and miserable to gather. I loved it. We usually took three or four days to gather it, but this was the last day, and we were down to the roughest, rockiest, brushiest part, where naturally, the smartest, wildest, nastiest cows lived. All winter, I kept these cows scattered like a madwoman's chickens to make the water last and avoid grouping them up in any one part.

I had the outside circle and was coming down a high ridge when the owner and his wife appeared below, about a quarter-mile away. They were riding along at a slow, snail's pace, smoking their Marlboros and not paying attention to anything in particular. I held up for a minute so I wouldn't get too far ahead of them, as they needed watching and were bound to get lost.

Soon, they split and rode on two sides of an oak thicket, still smoking, looking down country, and chatting away. They were about a hundred feet past the thicket when a black white-face cow poked her head out. She watched them ride away, then very quietly turned up country, taking her big unbranded calf with her. Needless to say, I met that cow and calf a little while later after a hard ride cross-country.

When I got to the holdup, I had 10 pairs I had picked up behind them. The owners were surprised I had found them.

The New Vet

Anyone who knows me well will tell you I hate squeeze chutes. But it seems I've spent half my life standing next to one, processing cattle at one feed yard or another, then at ranches, preg-checking cows, worming, or whatever. To quote an old friend, Leo Black, "The man who invented the squeeze chute didn't like to rope!"

Well, on this day, the new vet was coming to vaccinate some replacement heifers. I had spent the day before oiling, replacing parts, and tightening up a rickety off-brand chute. It had a guillotine headgate, which meant you had to open one side of the chute with a cable-pulled lever. The boss never took any interest in manual labor on the ranch, but today, he showed up, new Bailey hat, and new gloves.

The vet shows up, and I see why the boss is there. SHE is fresh out of vet school and fairly attractive in her form-fitting wranglers and tank top. We run the first heifer in, vaccinate her, and tag her. The boss rushes by me to the controls on the chute and, without saying anything, pulls the cable that releases the side door! With the heifer still squeezed in, it slammed the gate open, knocking the vet 30 feet onto her wrangler-wrapped butt.

The language that came out of her mouth! I looked up, and the boss was hot-footing it to his pickup, with the vet yelling obscenities at his back. Never had to worry about him getting in the way again!

Big Ole Button

This didn't happen to me, but it's such a good story, I gotta tell it. The fella who started me into punching cows was a big ole button from New Mexico who got a job on a big Arizona outfit packing grub to camps. In those days, everything was open, no fences, so there were lots of camps to keep cattle home. One camp set up in an isolated canyon, real lonely and remote.

Sam got into camp just at sundown, put his horse and pack string in the corral, and walked up to the tent the camp man used. The camp man was sitting outside pounding jerky for supper. He never knew Sam was within a hundred miles.

Sam slipped up behind him real quiet, reached around, and stole a piece of jerky. He still didn't see him. Sam stole another. The camp man still didn't know he was there. Sam laid his hand in the skillet and left it there.

The camp man looked down and damn near tore the tent down getting away. He ran a hundred yards before Sam tackled him!

Take Your Cows and Don't Come Back

Years ago, I had a ranch leased that was bordered on three sides by the Tohono O'odham Nation. I had to deal with four different grazing associations. Three were fine neighbors, as good as people I ever dealt with. I had the privilege of being the only white man to have permission to ride there. The fourth association, however, was stand-offish and solemn, almost hostile.

Between the smugglers and Border Patrol cutting fences, it was a full-time job checking fences and keeping the cattle home. After a big summer rain, I was riding the south boundary, checking water gaps. At an extra-large, deep wash, the fence was gone, and tracks were going both ways. I started tracking them south, hoping I would find them quickly before those war-like boys from that fourth association found me. The farther I went, the more trash I found—plastic, jugs, mason jars, etc.

Just as I found the cattle, we stumbled into a clearing. A sweet smell was coming from a big copper kettle with a hot mesquite fire under it. Four big, hostile Indian men stood staring at me like I had three heads! One stepped up, looked at my cows, looked at me, and said, "White man, take your cows and don't come back!" His hand was on a six-shooter.

In no time at all, all that was left of me there was the smell! I never said a word to anyone about that day, but that water gap had new wire the next day—and I didn't put it there!

My Rope is Still Rusty

Bob and I were helping Art work his rough, rocky central Arizona ranch. The only way you could work it was horseback—no vehicles, not even a four-wheeler. Breakfast was at 4, cooked on a wood stove, eaten by a kerosene lamp, and we'd leave an hour later, leaning out over the brow band. Many times, it was so dark you had to follow the sounds of the horse in front of you.

The cattle weren't bad, but in country that rough, you always got some snotty ones. This one morning, the wind was whistling, cold, with a hint of snow in the air. We were a good three hours from the house. We eased up on a ledge that overlooked a spring in a hole a quarter-mile below—a good hour's ride. As we rested our saddle seats, a string of cattle came into view below, single-file, on the way to water. Art studied the cattle through his long eyes (binoculars) and pronounced them long-eared.

"You boys stay here and catch what comes out," he said. "I'll go stir the pot with the dogs."

Art slipped off down the trail, followed by five dogs. When he stirred the pot, those dogs kept the cattle circling in that hole while Art caught and tied them down one after another! Bob and I looked at each other like a couple of fools.

Presently, we saw smoke down below as we eased up to the fire, we counted nine head tied down. The last two were tied with rope cut off from Art's catch rope! "I guess I made a pig of myself," he says! "I guess so," Bob says, "my rope is still rusty"!!!

The Day Donnie Smiled

Years ago, I helped my friend gather his ranch to settle his divorce. After his wife left, he sat in the house brooding for four years. Nothing got branded, nothing sold—it was just left to sit. But now, the judge was forcing him to work the ranch. He had to sell enough to pay off his ex. She already had some of the patented land, and now he had to give her cash.

We'd been gathering for a week, finding cattle he never knew existed. His demeanor seemed to change over time—from gloomy to a little chipper, even making a joke now and then. Even though he was down in the dumps, I enjoyed working with him. He was quiet and didn't like the crew being loud while working.

Everything was going well until one evening when we came into a brushy tank with a drive of 200 cows. We let them sift in, water, and then sift out the other side. Donnie, the ranch owner, and I were holding up the leaders when they came out the other side. When the drags came through into the open, there was the biggest crossbred steer I had ever seen. His horns had been sawed off years ago, and the brands had grown up into ridges on his sides. He belonged to the neighbors and was rank as a boot full of snakes!

I'd already jerked down the twine, ready for the wreck, but Donnie waved me off. I pulled up and just stared as that big sucker loped off up the country. Damn, I was mad. Donnie didn't say another word until we were feeding the horses that night. That steer had gotten away for nine or ten years, and we didn't have time to fool with him.

The next morning, as I was graining the horses in the dark, Donnie eased up and told me to catch my best pony today, then went inside to cook breakfast. When we went to saddle up, the boys from the next ranch were there. That's when Donnie told me that steer was back at that tank, and we were going after him.

I had an old thoroughbred crosshorse I called Knife. He didn't care how rough it got or how far he had to run to catch the forked-toed critter. His only problem was he wouldn't pull your hat off your head, but he would hold anything you caught.

When we got to the tank, it was just light enough to barely see. That old steer and a maverick cow were standing about 200 yards upcountry, right out in the open, big as life! As we cinched up, the cattle took off, heading upcountry. Donnie and I made a wild run but got them stopped and turned down country. The cow split off, and the old steer was rolling along like a Sunday freight train.

When my loop went around his stub horns, it ran through his eyes and blinded him as long as I kept it tight. We were heading downhill toward the trailers, so instead of stopping him, I let him lope along as we went in the right direction. I knew if I ever stopped that steer, we were done. When we reached the trailer, I stopped old Knife and let my dallies slip, turning that steer around at the back of the open trailer.

That steer was so strong, he just started backing, taking my rope as he went. He backed into the trailer clear to the front! We tied him, and by noon, he was in the Prescott sale barn, weighing in at 1,975 pounds— almost twice what old Knife weighed! Donnie smiled that day!

Hair-Raisin Stunts

I was helping my friend and neighbor, Lyman, in the Santa Maria Mountains. He was up in years and needed some help moving cattle from pasture to pasture. His granddaughter, Cathey, was helping—a skinny kid of 18 or 19. She worked at Old Tucson doing horse stunts and such. And, on top of that, she was a top hand for her age.

Lyman's wife, Allaire, had cooked us a great lunch, and we were sitting back enjoying another glass of tea. Lyman asked me if I would shoe a horse for him before I left. With a full belly, I agreed to do it. I hadn't noticed Cathey had left the room.

When I got to the barn to shoe the horse, there was Cathey with two broncs—and I mean broncs—tied together, riding them Roman style inside that low-roofed barn! As she ducked under the rafters at a trot, she explained it was a stunt she had to do for a show later that month. Roman riding in a barn, and she was practicing!

As the years went by, I watched her perform some hair-raising stunts with horses. She had more guts than you could imagine!

The Snottiest and Rankest

We had been gathering remnants off the 76 Ranch for a few months, and we were getting down to the snottiest, rankest cattle—those that continually got away or lived in the most inaccessible parts. My friend Wes had been helping for about three days, bringing his dogs, along with mine and Mrs. Jefe. Together, we'd made a pretty good drag. In the corral, ready to load and go to town, was a muley Brangus bull who was on the fight, and a horned crossbred cow, about a hundred years old. She didn't seem too bad as long as she was with gentler cattle.

We cut the bull and three gentler cows into the loading alley and ran them up into the trailer for the ride to the sale barn. The bull and cows ran up the chute and jumped into the trailer like saddle horses. Without shutting any gates behind us, Wes and I jumped into the trailer to shut the divider gate. Before we could, here came the crossbred cow behind us, right into the trailer! A mad fighting bull on one end and a mad fighting cow on the other, inside a covered trailer! For a minute, it was hell among the yearlings!

The tailgate to the trailer was two pieces that swung inside as well as out. Wes pulled half, and I pulled the other half inside, covering the corners, until those two old blisters went back down the alley. It took a little time to clean ourselves up and get back to loading those cattle—and not all the mess was on the outside of our wranglers!

Rockfish

Not too long ago, Manuel and I were tracking some wild cattle in the Weaver Mountains. He was riding a blue roan Navajo pony called Rockfish. That horse was hard to shoe, unpredictable, and a bit of a snake to get on, but he was a hell of a horse in rough country. The terrain was steep, rocky, and downright spooky in places. Manuel was in front, as he was the better tracker, when I saw him stop up ahead. The sign was getting fresher and greener, and I expected to come upon the cattle any time.

As I caught up to Manuel, I could see he was looking off the side of his horse, lost the trail. As I rode up, he turned in the saddle to speak to me. In front of him was a big, smooth boulder, five feet high, as smooth as a bowling ball. Just as Manuel started to speak, Rockfish jumped up on top of the boulder and balanced like an elephant on a beach ball!

Manuel started to shake, turned real slow, and said, "D-did y-y-you see that?" I nodded. Manuel slid off the right side and hit the ground, where his knees gave out. Rockfish hopped down and waited to regain the trail. It took Manuel a little longer to regain his composure!

Texans

In the early 70s, the International Feed Yard Team Roping Association got off the ground. The first finals were held in Vegas at an outdoor arena on Thanksgiving weekend, and it was a frozen mess. Hotel reservations were fouled up, and the weather never got above 30 degrees. Despite that, I managed to place in the mixed roping, earning a check and a new Resistol hat. Rex Allen did a concert in a big ole tent with about a hundred propane heaters trying to keep our steaks warm while we ate.

The next few years, the event was held in Elko, Nevada, at the Horse Palace indoor arena. It was still cold outside, but we were toasty inside! In the second year, I placed in the open roping, and in the third year, I qualified with two partners in the open roping. There were teams from Mexico, Canada, and Texas (that IS a foreign country, right?). Anyway, one of my partners won the world with another Arizona roper, and he and I placed third. Arizona ropers dominated the weekend.

In order to get your check, you had to attend a meeting where they took suggestions on how to improve the event. There were 20 Texans down front, arguing that we needed a cutting or calf roping, maybe even team penning. We said nothing, just wanted our checks and to leave. Eventually, the man running the meeting asked what we Arizonans thought. My partner smiled and said he didn't care about cutting, as we did that all day long at work.

A smart-mouthed Texan stood up and said, "Maybe you Arizonans ain't got nothin' that'll cut a cow."

With a smile, my partner replied, "Maybe not, but we damn sure can rope, huh!"

With that, 20 Texans stood up and turned around. We got our checks and left!

Lookin for Cows

I was helping my friend Bud gather and ship cattle from his ranch north of Phoenix in Cave Creek. His land was scattered all over, and the houses and ranchettes were creeping in, taking over a little bit at a time. Every pasture had its share of houses, yards, and dogs running loose, making things difficult.

One of the cowboys working with us was a Mexican man named Tony. He was a character in his own right, having ridden his own horse 20 miles just to get the job. His bedroll was a small Mexican serape, and his only other possession was a large bottle of tequila.

The roundup boss, Howard, liked to laugh at Tony and set him up for jokes. We were working a rough Malapai rock pasture one morning when Howard sent Tony off to work the top of a big, brushy ridge with some large trees on top. We had been holding up the cattle for about an hour when Tony returned with a small bunch of steers. He was unusually quiet, which wasn't like him. Finally, Howard couldn't take it anymore.

"What did ya see, Tony?" he asked.

Tony looked around at us, smiled, and said, "Lots of peoples there, no gotta any ropas (clothes). I told this naked lady, 'I'm lookin' for cows, Lady, not chee-chees!'"

It took us a while to get back to work after that!

Swearing to Buddha

I had been hired sight unseen by a couple of California steer speculators who planned to stock Arizona with 20,000 steers for the winter. My family and I had moved almost overnight from Wickenburg to Picacho, Arizona, to start receiving the cattle on the first of three ranches they had leased. All the arrangements had been made by these guys' banker. After three weeks, I still hadn't met the men, and they had handed me a checkbook and expense money, telling me to pay myself what I thought was fair.

They also instructed me to get a cell phone, one of the first I had ever used. It was a bag phone that lived in my pickup, and the reception was terrible.

One afternoon, while I was waiting for trucks to bring more steers, my bag phone went off. When I answered, it was one of my bosses, the ones I hadn't met.

"Is there a landing strip nearby?" he asked.

I told him where one was and drove there to meet him. It was a short strip used by crop dusters, with power lines on one end. Soon, a tri-cycle Beechcraft roared overhead at treetop height, circled, and came in over the power lines! When he touched down, the tail feathers barely missed the wires. He set it down on one wheel, skidded along for a few moments, then settled down on all three wheels, skittering down the strip. He did a U-turn in front of my pickup and landed like a spastic hen trying to land on a prickly pear nest!

The prop hadn't even stopped spinning when the side door flew open, and a very attractive brunette fell out on hands and knees, spitting four-letter words and calling my boss names that I had never even heard before.

I could hear him laughing as she swore to Buddha that she would *never* get in another airplane with him again!

Tropical Swamp Angels

After the boss had looked at all the Mexican steers we could find in the pickup and the brunette had cooled off, we stopped at a little roadside tavern for Coronas and lime. The boss laid a new one on me: he was sending me a bunch of Hawaiian heifers. OK, I'd had my fill of Floridian cattle, and the first thing that came to mind was more of those tropical swamp angels. I said so. But the boss assured me they weren't anything like Florida's gator bait. No Brahma, all English breeding, and, yes, they were trotty because Hawaiian cowboys don't do anything at a walk, but these cattle would get gentle with the right work.

It seems that the 50th state overproduces beef, and with a closed economy, they can't consume them fast enough, so they export them to the mainland. These cattle acclimated to Arizona really well, gaining almost four pounds a day on good alfalfa. And, yes, they were trotty. REAL trotty.

When it was time to ship these big, fat heifers with remnants of grass skirts, the boss impressed on me not to spend too much on shipping corrals (this pasture had NONE!) and to make it so we could pick it all up and take it with us when done. Me and two Latin American boys built a water lot, crowding alley, and sorting pens out of T-Posts and net wire! With a portable loading chute, we were in business.

When we had the corral full of cattle, we parked our pickups and trailers along the fence on the outside to keep the cattle from crowding the net wire. When a semi got there, we'd sort off a load and load the truck as we sorted. Never spilled a drop in three days of work, but that net wire corral was getting pretty ragged!

The second day was the only day we came close to a wreck. The boss was on one end of the alley sorting off a truckload. I was watching the gate behind him. The brunette and my wife were loading the alley. With the alley loaded, the brunette, who was wilder than an outhouse mouse, over-undered her horse and hollered at the boss that she was coming to help him! That brown pony went hurtling up the middle of the alley full of cattle, with the boss waving his hands and hollering to stop.

When she got up to him, not one heifer had jumped nor hit that wire fence! The boss, me, and my wife let out a long breath as the boss looked at me, smiled, and said, "Goooood fence!"

Let a Cowboy Do It

When I took over the 76 Ranch, we found there were a lot of ungathered remnants... and then we found out WHY! I have never, in my life, dealt with a more sour, spoiled bunch of good-quality cows. Fortunately, the boss had bought that great historic ranch with the brand. My wife and I found out real quick that these cattle would run until they fell over dead before they would let you hold them up. Some did! There were a couple bulls who, when reaching a certain point in the pasture, would just simply turn back over whoever was trying to hold them up. If you roped one, the Budweiser hitch couldn't move them! They had been roped and turned loose so many times, there was no leading them.

One bull, no matter where you were, would hide in the brush and then attack, trying to turn your horse over if he could. If he couldn't, he would give chase, hooking your horse in the butt for as long as a quarter mile! The one thing those cows respected was dogs. They'd been worked with heelers, and when a dog came around, they stopped to fight, knowing those dogs would chew on their heels or the calves. It was easy work for a bunch of young Catahoula catch dogs. Within a few months, we had thinned that bunch down to a handful of the oldest and worst.

Whenever we got a gooseneck load gathered, they went to the sale barn. Our only day off came on sale day. Being a stranger in this country, I didn't know many folks, so one day, at the sale, a package of those old renegades came in the ring. The previous owner, who was now living in a rest home, was sitting down front with his son-in-law. The son-in-law leaned over and told the old man, "See? They're stealing your cows!" The old man looked at his son-in-law and smiled, "I bought that ranch that way. I guess I can sell it that way! Besides, you had your chance and couldn't get 'em. Let a cowboy do it!"

Ned and Wiley

When I was at the 76 Ranch, I had the best dogs I've ever had: Catahoula-Border Collie crosses. The leaders were littermates, Ned and Wiley. No matter what you did, Ned was always out front of your horse, nose in the air, checking the breeze for cow smell. Wiley stayed behind, unless Ned picked up a scent. It was a pleasure to watch them work.

One spring morning, I was riding down a rocky trail to meet my wife at a windmill, about a mile away. Suddenly, I heard Wiley yelp. I looked back, and he was sitting there, holding one foot up with two drops of blood on it. A big rattlesnake was slowly slithering into the rocks. That sneaky snake had struck Wiley without a sound as I rode by. It was early enough in the spring that the mornings were still cool, almost cold.

I grabbed Wiley by the scruff of his neck and rode fast to the windmill with him in my lap. My wife saw me coming and knew something was wrong. At the windmill, I set Wiley down in the trough to cool off. After a few minutes, he stiffened, and I thought I was too late, but then he came around. Once he seemed better, I grabbed him and headed for the next windmill, where the truck was. Again, I put him in the cool water for a while. My wife loaded the horses and started the truck. We threw Wiley in the cab (dogs weren't usually allowed there), and began the 30-mile trip to the vet.

As we passed the house, we grabbed a sack of ice and continued on, with Wiley's foot packed in it. At the vet, she gave him two vials of anti-venom and said not to expect much. Two days later, she called to say to come pick him up. No ill effects or infection, and Wiley was back to work two days after that. Both Ned and Wiley are gone now. I don't think they would like not having cattle to work, so I guess it's for the best, but I still miss seeing those two work together, corralling those trotty old nellies.

Johnny Long

The story I'm about to tell happened back in the mid-'70s, one of about twenty similar incidents. I've never known this situation to end well, but for some reason, cattle owners keep trying it.

I was working at the Rafter Six ranch, one of three ranches my boss owned. He also had a feedlot. One of those ranches was the Battle Ax—a rough, cholla-infested place. The Gila River ran live for twelve miles along its southern border, but there wasn't a fence or any kind of boundary in sight. In the middle of the ranch stood a mesa with one narrow trail leading up and down, and almost no water at the top. All the trails were surrounded by cholla thickets, rocks, and mountain lions—a wonderful place to work, right?

One night, the boss called to say he had two truckloads of Brangus heifers to put on the backside of Bronco Mesa, at a windmill called Johnny Long. These heifers had been in the feedlot for 60 days to "warm up." I was to meet a couple of other punchers at the Battle Ax corrals, with my wife's little brother along. He was 14 at the time and had never worked cattle before, especially in this rough country.

When the trucks unloaded, it was clear these were farm cattle, not used to open country or cholla. When we opened the gates, the cattle had to make their way through a quarter mile stretch of cholla. Naturally, they panicked, stampeding through, each animal picking up cholla and passing it onto others like a chain reaction. The cattle scattered, each looking like black pincushions with cholla sticking to them. The farther they ran, the worse it got. There was no way to hold them up.

And then, it started snowing! In the next hour, it snowed, then rained, but the cattle were no closer to Johnny Long than I was to heaven. At one narrow spot, I looked around for my brother-in-law, but he was nowhere to be found. I asked one of the other boys, and they pointed down a rocky draw that even a mountain goat wouldn't attempt. Out of the draw came my brother-in-law, Bo, with five heifers in tow—him, his horse, and the cattle all covered in cholla but still upright.

By dark, we made it back to headquarters after getting about two-thirds of the cattle to the mill. The rest were scattered like a mad woman's chickens. Years later, I heard some of those grown-up heifers still ran wild there. And would you believe, I almost leased that ranch for the wild cattle there? Thank God my better half talked me out of it.

Aqui

When I was at the Rafter Six Ranch in Kearny, I had 250 acres of permanent pasture to irrigate. Every morning, I would go out and set the water to run on a 12-hour schedule, then do my ranch work until about 5 in the afternoon. After that, I'd set the night water to run until daylight the next morning.

I had a Mexican cowboy staying with us, and every evening, he would take my year-old son, Ty, and teach him Spanish. The big word was *aquí*—"here" in English.

One evening, I went out to change the water just at sundown and took Ty along. While I was working, I left him in the pickup, worried he'd get too close to a snake. When I went to leave, we realized the keys were gone! I asked Ty, and he kept saying "aquí," pointing out the window. The grass was almost knee-high, and I searched everywhere but couldn't find the keys. Meanwhile, Ty kept saying *aquí* and pointing.

Finally, I put Ty on my shoulders and started walking home, two miles away. I was mad, but I knew it was my fault for leaving the keys in the truck. When I got home, I called a friend, a good mechanic, to come put a new ignition in the truck.

The next morning, I saddled a pony and trotted back to change the water. As I stepped into the stirrup, I happened to glance down at the bed of the truck. In the

bed, right behind the cab, was a hole—and in that hole...
you guessed it... the key!

Buckeroos

Years ago, I had a ranch leased in Aguila, Arizona. It
had one big pasture of 45 sections, bordered by a huge,
ugly mountain on the north and a real fence on the south.
I had turned out 500 head of steers for a farmer who
wanted to try his hand at being a steer man. When it
came time to gather and ship, this farmer hired two
couples of buckeroos and sent them to me for help. They
had a good camp outfit and 8 head of big horses that,
anywhere else, would be pulling wagons full of tourists.

Every morning, these buckeroos would rope those
poor old ponies, which, with a little grain, could have
been caught without the fuss. The first morning, they all
turned out wearing Bermuda chaps (chinks). When I tried
to suggest they might want to get some proper chaps,
they made it clear they used these chinks everywhere
they went.

There was a pipeline that ran the length of the
pasture, right down the middle, with a drinker about
every mile and a half. As we left the corrals, I noticed my
wife's horse had a slight bob to his head, so I took it easy
until we reached the end of the pipeline. Along the way, I
could hear the buckeroos talking about our little desert
ponies. This was late May, and it was going to get hot
fast, but this bunch of meadow hay balers had no idea
what they were in for.

When we reached the end of the pipeline, I told my wife to take her time, work the pipeline, and look after her pony. The road ended there, and it was a good four miles to the back fence. As we left her, I kicked into a long trot. The temperature was already in the 90s. As I passed the buckeroos, I told them it was time to go and, if they were ready, to come on.

By the time we reached the back side of the pasture, those big horses were gasping for air, drenched in sweat. I scattered them out kind of thin and took the outside circle. When we returned to the corrals, my wife was waiting in the shade with about 100 head of steers, full and laying down. I added another 20 or so, and the four buckeroos had 5 between them. They also reported seeing more, but couldn't catch them because of the cactus!

These poor pilgrims were good, likable people, but like most buckeroos, they couldn't—or wouldn't—adjust to the ways of a different country. By the end, they had figured out that cattle can walk, that chaps really do work, and that not every horse needs roping. Our 1,000-pound ponies could get around the rough country and cactus; those monsters they rode couldn't.

Hula Hoop

When I worked for the Forepaugh Cattle Co. in Aguila, I had the chance to do a lot of things—and see a lot of things. Most of them made me scratch my head. Forepaugh ran 250 sections of pretty good desert country, mostly deeded land and state grazing leases, but if memory serves me right, the pasture called Summer Camp was BLM land. Just those three letters tell you all you need to know. Federal agencies are rarely helpful. Some individuals within them are good, honest people with common sense, but most of them couldn't pour piss out of a boot.

At the Forepaugh, we ran about four hundred mother cows and, when it rained, we'd turn out bunches of steers to take advantage of the feed. Summer Camp was used for those mother cows as a seasonal deal. It could have run a lot more cattle year-round, but the range conservationist put a stop to that. We could never get them to explain how they arrived at the numbers they allowed on that land.

One day, I was back there checking on the cows when I saw something strange. There was a guy wearing a sun helmet—like something you'd see in a Tarzan movie—shorts, a tee shirt with a rock and roll band logo on it, brogan boots, and high white socks. He had sunglasses on and a clipboard with some preprinted form, and in his hands, he was twirling a hula hoop.

Now, we were thirty miles from town, on a two-track dirt road, and here this guy was, playing with a hula hoop! His truck was parked back in the brush, barely visible. He hadn't noticed me yet, so I just sat on my horse, watching to see what this guy was up to. He was writing on the clipboard when I rode up, head down, studying that piece of paper. Then, all of a sudden, he tossed the hula hoop, and it landed on an ant hill about a hundred feet away. He marched over to it, knelt down, and started counting—one, two, three, and so on. I figured he was counting ants.

But before long, something told him someone was watching. He looked around, saw me, waved, and said, "Hi!" Then he marched over, hand outstretched. Without thinking, I reached out to shake it, only to see that he had a business card in his hand! I took it, and it said he was a range conservationist out of Phoenix.

"Nice to meet you," I said. "What are you doing?"

"Counting grass," he replied. "You throw the hoop, then count the plants inside it. That tells us how many cows can run here."

"But it landed on an ant hill!" I said. "No grass there. Why not over there where the grass is thick and solid?"

"Oh, that wouldn't be fair," he replied.

A week later, we got a letter cutting our permit in half. Now *that* wasn't fair!

Snake!!!

Anyone who knows me knows I can't stand the touch of a reptile—any reptile! Frogs, lizards, horn toads, snakes... I can't stand it! When my kids were little, they got great pleasure from chasing me around with a frog!

While working at the Forepaugh Ranch, the boss there had a routine that never varied. About 4 o'clock every day, Russ would grab a six-pack and head out to the Summer Camp well. He took enough gas to run the pump until the next day, around the same time. The road there was narrow, slow, and pretty rough, so Russ would idle along, sipping his beer as he went—except when he saw a snake. When Russ spotted a rattlesnake, he'd stop, grab his trusty shovel, and dispatch Mr. Snake, loading him in the back of the truck for a prank when he got home. I had gotten to the point where I was a bit jumpy around the barn and corrals, because Russ was always setting up a dead snake somewhere to scare me.

One summer afternoon, I'd been shoeing horses, and it got kinda late. It was just dark enough that you could still make out a person, but not much else. Russ was parked on the road I needed to take home, visiting with another driver when I pulled up. My wife and kids stayed in the truck while I got out to chat with Russ. I knew that meant drinking a beer and getting the report on the water situation at Summer Camp.

As I walked up, Russ swung his arm in a wide arc, and something long and round sailed through the air. Before I knew what hit me, it landed across my chest—a snake. The rattles were still buzzing as it hit the ground at my feet. I froze, unable to move. Russ strolled over, picked up the dead snake, and casually handed me a cold beer.

I told him, "If I could move, I'd choke you!" That snake had spattered blood all across my shirt and face! To this day, I can still smell that blood. My kids are still laughing about it!

Burro Creek

Times were tough. We had a roof over our heads, but no work. One afternoon, our friend Lyman stopped by the house and asked for some help. It seems he'd been to the hospital in Prescott to visit a friend when he met some folks who owned the old Loving U Ranch in the bottom of Burro Creek, outside of Bagdad. Well, Lyman knew no strangers, and struck up a conversation with these folks. They had a problem—about 20 cattle were running freely in Burro Creek!

Now, Burro Creek had live water year-round, and the BLM (Bureau of Land Management) was worried that those 20 head of cattle would destroy the fragile environment along the creek bottom. They demanded the cattle be removed immediately. The owners were nice folks with great educations but absolutely no knowledge of gathering cattle. So, Lyman contracted the gather on these cattle, but he needed help, and he knew I was looking for work. A deal was made.

A few days later, we pulled up to the edge of Burro Creek. What a sight! The road snaked down to the bottom at about an 8 percent grade over rock and clay. We unhooked our trailers on the top, with one man leading the horses, while Lyman and I drove our trucks down to the corrals and camping spot.

After setting up camp, staking the dogs (Lyman brought four), and eating a good supper, we went to bed in preparation for the next day's gather. Three men, four dogs, and six horses after 20 head in a canyon no wider than a half-mile at the widest? Piece of cake!

The next day, we made a good drag and got 18 head with the dogs doing the dirty work. We penned the cattle and were pleased with our good work. When the owner showed up that night with a bobtail truck to haul the cattle, he mentioned that he'd neglected to tell us there were two young bulls that also needed gathering. That made a grand total of four head. "Tomorrow they'll be in the corral," we bragged. Good cowboys, good horses, good dogs—what else could be the outcome?

That night, things took a downhill turn. The dogs got loose and got into the chuck box. The next morning, though not completely wiped out, we were short on grub. About ten o'clock that morning, we jumped the two cows that had been missing. Both had month-old calves and weren't keen on going to the corral. One pair headed toward the corral, and the other down the canyon. It took the whole crew to pen that one old Hereford cow and calf. Somewhere in the wreck, I spilled the last of my snuff, and when I went to the chuck box, I found the dogs had scattered my stash! In those days, being without Copenhagen was the same as being insane!

After a night with no nicotine and no coffee at breakfast (the dogs ruined that too), we set out after the remaining cattle. We decided that win, lose, or draw, we were out of there that night. Sure enough, we jumped the cow and calf, and as they dashed for the brush, I caught that old Nellie by the horns. While tying her to a tree, our third hand, Marty, came busting out of the brush, hot on the trail of the two bulls. There was a water-gap fence about a hundred yards away with a narrow gate. That gate was open. Just as the first bull went through the gate, Marty roped him, and the bull jerked Marty's horse sideways into the gate, blocking it. The second bull was trotting along the fence looking for a hole when we caught up to him. At the sight of us, the bull ran up to a point overlooking a large pool of water. There, the bull turned to fight. The dogs took to him, and he dove into the pool with a dog on each ear. All three disappeared under the water!

I was about to follow, then decided against it—after all, it wasn't Saturday! When the bull surfaced, there was a dog on each side, and they took after him again. When they came out of the water, I was waiting and caught the bull, tying him to a gentle cottonwood tree. By now, I was getting pretty irritable with no Copenhagen! Marty and Lyman were staying out of the way, not saying much. We necked the bulls together, blindfolded them, and drove them to the corral. Along the way, I picked up the cow and led her in, all the while getting crankier and crankier!

When we loaded up, Marty, without a word, grabbed the horses and started up the road while Lyman and I spun our tires all the way to the top of the canyon. Hooked up, loaded, and rolling, we made Bagdad in about two hours over rough road. Lyman pulled over and went into the Quik Stop, coming back with a cold beer for each of us and a bonus for me—a can of Copenhagen! Nothing was better! A couple of hours later, I was home with a check, a fresh can of snuff, and a smile on my face!

Tyson

I had a friend, Art, who lived in the Artillery Peaks with his wife, Patsey, on a ranch she had inherited. The ranch had been in her family for three or four generations, and it was a beautiful place—one road in and no other access. If you wanted to get around, you had to be on horseback. The old pack trail from Wickenburg to the mining town of Sentinel ran through the property, cutting through solid rock. That trail had been worn a foot deep, just wide enough for a mule or horse to pass.

Art worked the ranch with Patsey and her sister, rarely hiring help. I got to help them a few times, and it was always a treat. Patsey cooked on a wood stove, and let me tell you, it was good. The water came from a spring, funneled into the house through a half-inch pipe in the wall, ending with a faucet over a bucket with a dipper. The bunkhouse, down in the creek bottom, was spotless. Lanterns provided the light, though there were a few kerosene lamps in the main house. The heat came from a fireplace and the cook stove. The adobe house stayed cool in the summer if you left the windows open.

Art used a lot of dogs, especially catch dogs, since many of his cattle were a bit tough to handle on your own. His main dog at the time was a big red merle named Tyson, after a friend's son.

One day, we were out looking for an old wild cow that Art wanted to sell at the auction. We rode for hours, hopping from pinnacle to pinnacle, searching the highest, most inaccessible areas of the ranch. Finally, Art stopped, got off his horse, and pulled out his binoculars. After about ten minutes, he quietly said, "There she is." Following his finger across the canyon, I saw a red spot on a ledge.

After riding for another hour, we reached the ledge. It was about ten feet wide and maybe sixty feet long. There, at the far end, lay the old cow—drooling, her eyes sunk deep into her skull. She was done for. She heaved herself to her feet, but as soon as she saw us, she went on the offensive. Before we could react, Tyson raced past, grabbed the cow by the nose, and held on tight. Tyson weighed about 100 pounds, and the cow was probably 700. As the cow backed away, dragging the dog with her, she bawled in protest. Tyson stayed set, pulling against the weight of the cow.

Art shook his head and, barely above a whisper, called Tyson's name. The dog opened his mouth, and in that instant, the cow lost her balance, falling over the cliff. She died instantly.

Art sat there, rolled a cigarette, then turned his horse back toward the house. "Chalk up one for Tyson," was all he said.

Ole Dave

I was working for Dave down at Alamo Lake. He had about a thousand steers turned out on the desert there. Alamo Lake was fenced off up to what was called Three Rivers at Brown's Crossing. The Big Sandy and the Santa Maria rivers come together to form the Bill Williams River, which flows a whole three miles into the lake. Brown's Crossing was where the rivers met, and all that was left were giant, old, dead cottonwood trees. Dave's steers weren't supposed to be around the lake or in the Three Rivers area.

One night, the park ranger came to the ranch to tell us that some fishermen had left the gate open, and a bunch of steers had gotten into Three Rivers. There was a gal camping there, watching some bald eagles that were nesting in the dead cottonwoods. She was worried that one of the eagles might fall out of the nest, and the steers would step on it. Dave assured her that the eagles wouldn't hurt the steers, but she didn't see the humor in that. He told them we would be there the next morning at daylight to gather the steers. What no one knew was that

Dave had opened that gate. The waters were drying up on the desert, and those steers needed to drink from the lake and river.

Of course, the environmentalists and fishermen couldn't stand that—the cow manure in the water and pee on the trails!

The next morning, five of us unloaded our horses on the bluff overlooking Brown's Crossing, and sure enough, those steers were bedded around the old cottonwoods. The river here is notorious for quicksand—not like you see in the movies, but it will bog a horse or cow, sometimes really deep.

When we all cinched up, Dave said in a whisper that sounded as loud as a bullhorn, "You all wait here. I'll find us a crossing." He rode down to the riverbank, rode up and down three times for effect, then turned and said, "We can cross here, be quiet!" With that, he rode old Punkin into the river and bogged him down to the saddle skirts!

"@#$@#$!" Dave yelled as old Punkin rolled over on him, mashing down into the sand and water! When Dave yelled, those steers took off like the hounds of hell were after them! Bob went by Dave on one side, and I went by on the other, at a dead run. Dave was cussing and digging sand and mud out from under his glasses and hat, leading a waterlogged Punkin back to dry land. Those steers tore up the river bottom as they ran.

There was no way to turn them, so Bob and I went back up the bluff. As we got there, the ranger was saying, "See, Annie? Old Dave put those steers right where he wanted them!" Bob looked at me and said, "A dunk in the river was a cheap price for watering those steers!"

Horse Tracks and a Runnin Iron

You know, for my whole life, small ranchers and town ranchers have always been suspicious of a man who gets up before daylight, already five miles out, looking over the brow band. I guess it's because they think, if you're not sitting in the coffee shop with them, there must be something wrong with you! Those folks who think the coffee shop can't survive without their daily business just seem to believe they're more important than the rest of us. Every time I spent any time in those shops, it seemed like they knew more about everyone else's business than the people they were talking about.

Then you've got brand inspectors. They're a valuable asset to a cowman, but their self-image can get in the way. Pin a badge on one, and suddenly everyone is a suspect. As they move from ranch to ranch, inspecting brands, they gossip like fertilizer spreaders. So while you're out there making horse tracks and minding your own business, those coffee shop stool polishers are spreading rumors about you.

Years ago, I worked on the 76 Ranch. The place was a mess—years of poor management had left it in bad shape for the new owner. The corrals were falling apart, water wells wouldn't pump, and tanks hadn't been cleaned in years. In my limited experience, the only way to fix that kind of mess is to pull your hat down and get to work.

My neighbor to the east was an old puncher spending his last years working a little ranch for an absentee owner. Bill had worked the river and crossed the mountains. He was a hand, through and through.

The neighbor to the west was a big, loudmouth ex-football player who had owned a dozen ranches but never stayed on one long enough to even find the horse corral. He spent all his time at the coffee shop or in the USDA office trying to find some free government money. His cows never seemed to produce enough calves, but then again, with old bulls and not enough of them, what did he expect?

Thursday was sale day, and a lot of ranchers went to town for the auction. Bill was there one day after unloading his calves, having coffee in the café at the sale barn. The bigmouth football player was sitting there with him. Bill asked him how he could spend all his time in town knowing his neighbor was out riding every day, carrying a running iron, with ten miles of bad fence between their two ranches. The football player spewed coffee all over the table, got up, and stormed out of the café. Bill was laughing so hard he almost couldn't breathe, but then he realized he got stuck with the check!

Peaches

Why is it that when you're running a ranch for a dude, they always want to bring all their town friends to help? Most of them are nice people, well-meaning, but they just get in the way. When I was younger, I didn't have much patience for those folks. Maybe that's why I didn't stay anywhere too long. But as I got older, I became more tolerant. They can't help it if they didn't have the kind of education we did. They spent all their time being lawyers, doctors, and such, while we learned a far more important trade: feeding the country. But we had dirt under our fingernails, so...

Anyway, we were branding at the 76. We were short-handed, so I had to put up with a couple of town folks who had been invited by the owners. Honestly, they were better help than the owners themselves. As the day went on, we got into the rhythm and started getting things done. One of these town folks was a little uppity, but not too bad. When we stopped for lunch, I noticed him turn his nose up at the bill of fare. But he did get a plate and nibbled at the lunch my wife had made for the crew, who were scarfing it down.

We had an ice chest full of cold drinks and cans of fruit for dessert. I had a can of peaches and was sitting on the edge of the water trough, spearing peaches out of the can with my knife when this prissy feller asked, "Is that the same knife you use all day castrating bulls and ear-marking calves?"

I nodded and rolled a peach to the other side of my mouth, replying, "Yeah, but..." Hell, he was already puking down on his hands and knees! I was going to tell him I washed it first, but I changed my mind.

Pay Attention!

At the 76 Ranch, we turned the weaned calves back out to grow into yearlings, trying to make 600-pounders out of them. We were understocked, so we always had extra feed. I kept one pasture just for the calves, so it was always in good condition.

The owner wasn't one for physical labor, but he liked Mrs. jefe's cooking and would come out to ride with us when we gathered cattle or yearlings. He didn't try to give orders, which made him easy to work with. I kept his horse shod and ready for whenever he felt like joining us—which wasn't often.

That fall, the yearlings did exceptionally well. The summer rains had filled the tanks, and the gramma grass was waist high. The mesquite bean crop was heavy, and those black baldie yearlings, instead of weighing 600 pounds, were closer to 700! I consigned two truckloads to a special stocker sale in November. I ordered trucks for the Wednesday before the sale, then called my friend Wes to help gather the cattle Monday and Tuesday and load them out on Wednesday.

When Wes showed up on Monday morning, the owner followed him through the gate—he wasn't going to miss Mrs. jefe's breakfast. The pasture was about 15 sections, mostly flat, with a southern drainage. The north half wasn't as thick with brush as the south, so we worked the southern half first, throwing the cattle north of the road into a dirt tank to settle them and water out. The road split the pasture east to west, and you could see far into the north, where one man could cover a lot of ground alone. I sent Wes up north to handle that, and we started moving the cattle down the road to the shipping pens. I told everyone not to let those yearlings wander south of the road, or we'd lose them in the thickets.

The first two miles went smoothly. Mrs. jefe took the drags, the owner rode the swing, and I had the point. As we crested a rise, I noticed Wes was about a mile above us, trying to turn a bunch of cattle that weren't cooperating. The drive was strung out, moving along like milk cows headed for the corrals. I hollered at the boss and told him to keep the cattle like they were, and I'd go help Wes. He nodded as if he understood.

I loped up to Wes, and between the two of us, we got the cattle turned and headed for the corrals. There was a lane about a mile long leading to the pens, and our group arrived just as the leaders from the main drive reached the gate. It was smooth sailing from there. But when we got back to the ranch that night, I asked Mrs. jefe what had happened with the cattle on the south side.

She explained that as soon as I was out of sight, those yearlings started crossing the road into a thicket. The owner, smoking his Marlboro and gazing at the clouds, let them scatter. Mrs. jefe took off through the thicket to round them up and turned them back. She told the owner to "pay attention or no more biscuits for breakfast!" The owner later told me that she came by him like a pay wagon passing a tramp, ordering him to put out the cigarette and focus on the job!

Donkey Catchers

Many years ago, a wise bureaucrat decided there were entirely too many donkeys in the Grand Canyon. He convinced the higher-ups to fund an expedition to gather these donkeys and relocate them to Alamo Lake. Now, I don't know if anyone really knew how many donkeys were in the canyon, but an enterprising puncher figured there were plenty. And if there weren't, he'd make sure there would be!

Sure enough, that puncher got the contract to gather the little fellers that had been wreaking havoc on the environment of the 7th Wonder of the World. He convinced the Feds they needed a helicopter to spot the burros, and about five men to give chase and rope them. Then he needed an extensive set of panel corrals and a truckload of hay to hold and feed the donkeys until they could be shipped to Alamo Lake. Every morning, a bobtail load would go out, and at Alamo Lake, a Fed would unload and count the little fellers.

But what nobody knew was that there was a second crew of cowboys at the lake who would re-gather the donkeys, load them up, and haul them back to the canyon at night to release them! Before it was over, some of those donkeys, when roped, would just turn and run to the truck, jump in, and wait for the ride. The upshot was that the puncher who came up with the idea made enough off the deal to buy a pretty good little ranch—thanks to the Fed!

Suzy the Dog

When I was just a button—about five years old—my dad took a job at a ranch along the Agua Fria River. The camp we had was old and isolated, just a few yards from the river. I remember that old adobe house with big, high ceilings. When we moved there, there was an old yellow dog lying on the screen porch. She came to us wagging her tail and looking for a pet. There was a note on the door that said her name was Suzy, and it would be best to keep her around because she warned of snakes. Now, I don't remember all this, but my mom told the story many times.

Suzy became my best friend and companion. When I went with Dad to milk the cow, Suzy was always in front on that rocky trail to the corral. Many times, she would point out a snake by the trail. She'd circle the snake, barking and howling, until Dad got there to deal with Mr. Snake. There was a barbed-wire fence along the road, and I remember Dad hanging up the snakes he killed on that fence—more than anyone can remember.

At night, many times, we'd wake to Suzy barking and carrying on out in the yard. Dad would get up, kill the snake, and we'd go back to bed. She'd even point out scorpions and centipedes crawling up the walls. I don't remember how long we lived there, but I know Mom was about to pull her hair out over the snakes. I started school there in a one-room school and rode a little yellow bus to the back. I was the only one in the first grade, along with a little blonde-haired girl. We even had a Christmas play, which I still remember.

Dad found another job in Maricopa, where he stayed the rest of his life. But we always remember Suzy, who we left there for the next folks to come along. I was worried about her getting fed, but Dad said the ranch owners took care of her. Not many folks get friends like her.

Baggy Pants and a Rattlesnake

A few years ago, we moved to Bowie and bought an old cotton farm. We weren't planning to farm cotton, but it had good fences, a nice house, and a barn—perfect for keeping a few cattle and our horses. But like all old farms, it came with a big scrap pile of junk: worn-out farm equipment, broken implements, and scrap metal. A real mess.

After we got settled in, I set about cleaning it up. A day or so into the task, I realized it was going to take more work than I had originally thought. After a few phone calls, I came up with a plan that would not only clean up the mess but also make a few bucks.

I contacted a scrap recycler in Tucson who was willing to bring a semi-trailer and park it at our place. All I had to do was load it up, and they'd haul it away and send me a check. It sounded like a perfect deal.

As I began the chore, I quickly realized there had to be a nest of rattlesnakes nearby. I killed about a dozen in the first week. After a couple of weeks of steady work, I had the trailer nearly full but still had another load or two left to go. They brought me an empty trailer, picked up the full one, and I was back at it. I had a little ranch leased nearby, so I had to take time to look after it, too. Between that and finishing loading the second trailer, it took me a little longer, but eventually, I got it done.

When I called the scrapyard to have the second trailer picked up, they told me their truck was broken, but they'd send a contract trucker. The trucker showed up—a young fellow who was pleasant enough, though his pants were sagging so low they were nearly dragging on the ground.

I showed him where the trailer was and then went back to shoeing a horse. Shortly after, I looked up and saw the kid running around wildly, waving his arms. I could hear faint shrieks coming from his direction. I jumped in the pickup and sped over to see what was going on.

When he saw me coming, he came running toward me, flailing his arms over his head and yelling that something was chasing him! I thought he was having some kind of hallucination, until I saw it—a two-foot rattlesnake had struck at him and gotten its fangs caught in the baggy cuff of his pants. The snake was stuck, buzzing angrily as the kid danced around.

I grabbed him by the arm and led him over to the truck to get a shovel. Meanwhile, the snake was still writhing, and the kid was panicking. I tried to chop the snake's head off with the shovel, but after three attempts, I finally managed to do it.

The kid collapsed on a nearby stump, breathing hard, and I cut the rattles off to give to him. He wouldn't take them. It took him a full hour to calm down enough to drive back to Tucson. After that, I bet he was sure to hitch up his pants properly!

Tennis Shoe and Old Jello

Our neighbor Lyman needed help gathering a herd of Barzona cows from the 90-section DG Ranch. The terrain was rough and steep, with deep, brush-filled canyons. It was late August, and help was scarce, so I brought my horses and our two preteen boys along.

Lyman had a full-time cowboy and a couple of Latin American riders who could handle a horse. One of the younger Mexicans had an unpronounceable name, so Lyman just called him Tennis Shoe. He turned out to be a good hand, always willing to take on any task. He could build rock walls without mortar, perfect and sturdy.

We started gathering, but it wasn't going to be easy. It was hot, and in the afternoons, monsoon rains drenched us. What we hoped would be a one-week gather was turning into three. The cattle were scattered, and with puddles of water everywhere, they weren't congregating at the windmills. Some days, we'd work ten sections and only get 20 cows—if we were lucky.

Now, I'm not particularly fond of Barzona cows, but in this case, they were the right fit. The ranch had plenty of small, flat-topped mesas, and those red cows would hide under the cap rocks, where no other critter dared to venture. Of course, that made getting to them difficult— steep and shaly, and dangerous at times.

One morning, Lyman asked me to shoe the horse Tennis Shoe rode. We all called the pony "Yellow," but Tennis Shoe called him "Jello." When Jello lost his shoe, he lost part of his quarter hoof wall, so I built a shoe with an extra-long trailer to cover the broken spot.

Once done, we started our trot to the back of the circle, out beyond a few of those steep mesas. Lyman split the crew up, and as he rode along, he mentioned a particular mesa that was steep and covered with thorny Palo Verde and Mesquite. Tennis Shoe was dropped off next to last, leaving just me to finish the encirclement.

Lyman pointed high, and I could just make out the hindquarters of a cow behind a tree. That's where I was headed. The cow tracks were thickening, indicating more cattle. As I climbed higher and higher, it became nearly impossible for my horse to stand. I finally hobbled him in a flat spot and set off on foot.

When I reached where the cow should've been, all I found were deep tracks, fresh manure—and a horseshoe with an extra-long trailer. Below, I spotted a string of red cows winding down a trail, with a dun horse following, ridden by the skinny Mexican kid, Tennis Shoe, whooping it up on him!

Tom Was a Duffass

When we lived in Aguila, we were neighbors with a family that owned a large piece of land. They ran some cows, and if it rained, they'd stock feeder steers. The father was a good man, though he'd lost part of his arm at some point, which didn't slow him down at all. He was always busy with some project on the ranch. At the time I met him, he was also battling cancer in his back.

His son, Tom, was freshly married to a nice woman, but Tom was an accident waiting to happen. I've never met anyone who had as many wrecks as that guy. One evening, he went to the corrals to feed the stock. When he didn't return after dark, his wife went looking for him with a flashlight. She found him staggering home, the side of his head bloody and swollen. Turns out, he had climbed to the top of a haystack to feed the cows when he got his spurs caught in a bale wire and flipped 25 feet to the ground. Knocked out and with his scalp torn open, he had laid there for a couple of hours while the cows walked over him.

Another time, he asked me to help them brand some calves that had missed in the works. When I arrived, I found they planned to put the calves through a squeeze chute designed for full-grown cows. It wasn't made to adjust for smaller animals, but Tom insisted we use it anyway. I found out later that Tom couldn't throw a rope down a well, let alone catch a cow.

We started branding, having done about 20 head when a small black heifer came into the chute. There was no way to hold her—the headgate wouldn't close tight enough, and the squeeze wouldn't pinch her. Tom came to the headgate and asked me to open it so he could grab her and flank her.

As I opened the gate, Tom swung it wide and ducked into the chute, ready to meet the heifer head-on. She was ready. She hit him in the chest, knocked him over, and walked the length of him while he wrapped his arms around her neck, bucking and bawling on top of him. He finally let go just as I grabbed her by the tail, walked up her side, and flanked her.

I looked back to see Tom on his hands and knees, blood dripping from a tear in his scalp. His wife walked by with syringes to vaccinate the heifer. She didn't even slow down but did ask if he was okay, never even looking at him. His old father shook his head as he branded the heifer, saying, "Tom grew up on the ranch but didn't learn enough to fill a thimble!"

Asleep at the Switch

Tom was a neighbor—nice guy, but a bumbling fool. He needed help gathering a mountain pasture, so my wife, a couple of other cowgirls, Tom's dad, and I headed out. The pasture was rough—steep, rocky, and full of cactus. At the base of the main canyon, there was a small, spring-fed pond. That would be where the trouble started.

We left my wife and one of the other gals at the pond to catch any cows we drove down to them. Our plan was to be out by one in the afternoon, and with a five-mile drive to the corrals, that was ambitious enough.

Tom, his dad, a friend of Tom's, and I went up the canyon—two on each side of the stream. Near the summit, the stream became un-crossable. Tom and his friend were on one side, while Tom's dad and I were on the other. We agreed that no one would start down until we were all together.

We finished gathering our side of the canyon and waited for Tom and his friend. It was getting later than planned, and we needed to move on. Still no Tom. Eventually, Carl, Tom's friend, came over to the canyon's edge and yelled down. He said Tom had left on foot about two hours ago to push some cows out of the canyon but hadn't returned.

We drove our cattle down to the girls at the pond, then went back up to look for Tom. Carl had Tom's horse, and he said Tom had left it behind. Tom's dad was really worried. Everyone knew Tom was accident-prone, and we all imagined him lying somewhere with a broken leg or worse.

We searched the canyon, calling out and climbing the rocks until nearly dark. Finally, Tom's dad suggested we check by the pond. As we made our way down, the first person we saw was my wife, her Italian temper already past boiling.

"THAT LAZY, GOOD-FOR-NOTHING S.O.B. IS ASLEEP UNDER A MESQUITE TREE BELOW THE POND!" she yelled. "WHEN I WOKE HIM UP AND TOLD HIM YOU WERE LOOKING FOR HIM, HE SAID, 'DON'T WORRY, THEY'LL GIVE ME UP FOR DEAD SOON!'"

Tom didn't know how close he was to being dead himself. His dad gave him an earful, the other cowgirl chewed him out because she was supposed to be home hours earlier, and my wife would have cut his throat right there if I'd loaned her a knife.

By the time we got to the corrals, it was three hours later, and we had to put 90 cows in by moonlight. Our kids were home alone, thank God they were responsible. Our horses were tired, and we hadn't eaten since four that morning.

We swore never to go back, but, as it usually goes, the old man talked us into it one more time. A few weeks later, we headed out again to help—but that's another story.

Tom's Big Roundup

Tom had pastured a couple hundred cows for a friend of mine. My friend asked if I would go there and help gather these cows, even though I wasn't crazy about working with Tom. The Mrs. and I went. For three days, we worked this great big pasture, putting our gather in a holding trap every evening. By my count, we were only short about 20 cows when we started work on the fourth day. My wife swore up and down that we had gathered a lot of these cows twice. I wasn't sure of that, but she always had a better memory for individuals than me.

Once again, we scattered at the back of a long, rectangular pasture and started working back toward the trap. Once again, we were picking up large bunches of cows. Something was wrong. These cows were getting almost impossible to drive. Instead of going west to east, they would run north to south. I had left Mrs. Jefe on the south edge of the drive on a damn good mount, so I knew there wouldn't be a screw-up.

About halfway through the drive, I saw a pickup boiling toward me from the south. A fellow was in the back, waving at me and yelling. Damn hunters, I thought. When they got there, they told me the Mrs. had had a wreck and was hurt. It was two miles down to where she was, so I tied my horse and rode down to where she was with the hunters. Her horse was tied close, and the horn and forks of her saddle were packed in dirt and greasewood. She was sitting, propped up against a mesquite tree in the shade, obviously in great pain.

She had been trying to turn a goofy old cow and hadn't seen a low mesquite tree. Her horse had seen it and tried to jump it, hanging his front feet in the top of the little tree. This caused a cartwheel, with the Mrs. underneath the wheel! We loaded her in the truck, drove to our truck, changed rides, and I headed to the hospital 30 miles away.

While there, the hunters gathered up my horses and took them to the corrals for us. I never even got their names or saw them again. Not all hunters are stinkers.

At the hospital, we found out she had a broken collarbone. A wrap, a sling, and some pain pills, and we headed home. That night was a booger. The kids didn't like my cooking, the Mrs. couldn't get comfortable, and every move hurt. All the while, she kept telling me that the cow she was driving at the time of the wreck was a cow she had gathered two times before.

Tom came to the house and said we had all the cows gathered and would ship the next morning. The Mrs. assured me she would be okay, told me to go, and quit fussing over her.

The next morning, five of us set about gathering the trap, as the trucks were to be there at noon. There were lots of tracks of the cattle, but the farther we rode, it was evident there weren't any cattle in the trap! Soon, I heard a yell over to my right, so I loped over there. One of the other riders was sitting on his horse, looking at about a hundred yards of laid-over fence with a trail a foot-deep and a yard-wide going over it!

Tom rode up and looked at it and, in a whipped voice, explained the fence had been up the last time he checked it. His dad asked when that was. "Last year," he whimpered.

Tom looked at his 75-year-old dad, with one arm and a cancer growing in his back and ask him to go get some posts and fix the fence!! The rest of us turned our horses and headed back to the trailers. I heard Tom's dad say, in a firm voice, for Tom to fix the fence or he would call off the trucks and call the cows owners. I don't know what would have been worse, making excuses for a pitiful excuse of a son or fixing the fence.

ROPIN'

Stepped on My Eyes

1970, Mormon Lake roping, 4th of July. I'm batching out of the bed of my pickup, got coffee on the Coleman stove, horses fed, cooking breakfast. My friend, who is a Babbit cowpuncher, is still asleep in his teepee. But with the smell of the coffee, he crawls out on his hands and knees. When I hand him the coffee, he looks up with two black eyes! Knowing there had been a wild dance at the lodge the night before, I ask the question, and he replies, "Someone stepped on my eyes!"

I Run Real Fast

My friend, Dean, had just gotten married. I had just gotten divorced. We were all at a cookout and roping/playday—just a good time Saturday afternoon among friends and classmates. One of the events was ribbon roping. For those who don't know how it works, a ribbon is rubber-banded to a calf's tail. The roper catches the calf, and a girl runner pulls the ribbon and runs to the finish line—fastest time wins. Dean's new wife came to me and asked if I would rope a calf for her. I paid the entry fee, and we entered.

When our turn came, I roped the calf quick, was halfway down the rope, when this blonde streak went by with the ribbon in hand! We won hands down. Turned out, she was a sprinter for the ASU women's track team! "Ringer!" all the folks yelled as we counted the winnings! When she asked me to rope, she simply said, "I run real fast." Then, when she picked up the winnings, they gave her a little bitty first-place ribbon with about $200 in cash. She brought it back and said all she wanted was the ribbon! I think Dean choked on his beer!

Empty Stash

In the early '70s through the '80s, rodeo producer/promoter Bill Roer produced what he called the Rope-a-thon—eight days of roping at his place in Laveen. The arena seemed like it was a quarter mile long, with a 25-foot score. Big, hard-running steers made it a challenge.

One of the most popular ropings was the feedlot event. Only feedlot employees or owners could rope. In those days, there were plenty of feedlots and cowboys who roped. Dude was a friend of mine who worked at the same feedlot as I did. His wife was a moderating factor in his life, or he would have been like the rest of us: harum-scarum with our money.

Dude had been saving his shekels for months so he could go to Roer's. On the day the entries were due, he went home to get his cash. When he went to check his stash, he found it empty. Going to his wife with the empty sock, she merely pointed to the laundry room at a new washer and dryer. "That's yours and Roer's," she said! Dude didn't get to go that year!

Partner Joe and I

Partner Joe and I worked together at a couple of feed yards. We also roped together at the feedlot ropings and open events. We had been on a good three-year roll, placing about everywhere and winning a few. We didn't know it at the time, but people were calling us "those feedlot assholes!" We seemed to have a habit of coming from behind to place.

We were at a feedlot roping in Maricopa when it got down to the short go. I had legged our first steer and didn't think we'd get a call in the short. I had pulled the wood off my pony when Joe loped up and hollered we'd get a run! I resaddled and loped my cold horse back to the arena. Joe was already in the header's box when I got there.

When in the heeler's box, I looked at Joe, and he was grinning at me. I had seen that before and knew what it meant. He nodded and threw 30 feet of rope, 32 feet, and ducked. One blind swing at the corner, and the clock stopped at 5!! That's when the announcer (along with a lot of whiskey) called us "assholes!" We split second and third!

Old-Time Rodeo Hand

Years ago, when I was an aspiring team roper, there was an old-time rodeo hand in Casa Grande who owned a bar. There was another roper there who shall remain nameless (he's still with us) who bet the old-timer he could rope 10 muley steers without a time limit and without a miss. The time was set, and lots of side bets were made. The original bet was a lot of money for that day and time. The night of the event, the whole team roping community turned out to watch.

The old hand climbed up on the fence to watch and heckle the roper. There was no time limit set, so when the first steer was turned out, the roper casually loped the steer to the bottom of the arena, then followed it around until the steer began to trot. At that point, he stood up in his stirrups, took dead aim, swung three times, and MISSED!!! A collective groan went up from the crowd! We all decided drinking beer would be more interesting that night!!!

I told him I charged twice what anyone else charged. That didn't make any difference. I was under this horse's hind leg when he kept on about how I ought to ride this horse for him. I pointed to an empty corral with my hammer and said, around a mouthful of nails, "Put her there, and if you miss one payment, I'll keep your horse." I put my head down, nailing on the shoe. Pretty soon, I heard his truck start and drive away.

In the corral, he left a four-year-old black-and-white paint mare. And I NEVER saw that gentleman again. That mare made a whumpus kitty rope horse that I rode to many a set of heels in the junior rodeo circuit. When I finally sold her, she kept on giving, as she helped keep Carter in school for another semester.

Get **Ready, Big Boy**

Years ago, when we lived in a town with a great ropin' club, Mrs. Jefe was in the lead for a series ropin' saddle. We were right down to the end, and the points were close between Mrs. Jefe and a good friend who was a local businessman. When the ropin' started, Herb and Mrs. Jefe were partnered up pretty evenly. Thank God El Jefe was only ropin' with one of them!

When it came to the short round, only 2/10 of a second separated the two. Herb was to go first, and he and his partner made a good, solid run. When he came back, he said, "If I let a woman beat me tonight, I'll quit ropin'!"

As Mrs. Jefe rode by on her way to the box, she said without looking right or left, "Well, get ready, big boy. You're about to sell out."

Herb didn't win the saddle, but he didn't sell out either!

Paint Mare

Years ago, we rented the property where George Ara's arena is now. We were there to receive and care for Mexican steers that were being pastured on three different ranches in Pinal County. We didn't have any help, just me, Mrs. Jefe, and three teenage kids. The steers came every night from Nogales, Douglas, and Sasabee. We didn't get a lot of sleep.

One afternoon, when I had 15 minutes I wasn't needed somewhere, I was trying to tack a shoe on a pony who wasn't a lot of fun to shoe. It was during the big Indian Rodeo in Casa Grande when a truck and trailer pulled into the yard. An Indian fellow got out, introduced himself, and told me who he was.

He said he had a colt and wanted me to ride and train the horse. Well, I knew this Indian fellow by reputation. While he was a great silversmith, he had a bad habit of not paying what he owed.

I told him I didn't have time to ride his horse, but thank you anyway. He wouldn't take no for an answer, and he insisted and wouldn't leave. I told him that I charged twice what anyone else charged. That didn't make any difference. I was under this horse's hind leg when he kept on about how I ought to ride this horse for him. I pointed to an empty corral with my hammer and said around a mouthful of nails, put her there if you miss one payment I'll keep your horse. I put my head down, nailing on the shoe. Pretty soon, I heard his truck start and drive away.

In the corral, he left a four-year-old black and white paint mare.

And I NEVER saw that gentleman again. And that mare made a whumpus kitty rope horse that I rode to many a set of heels in the junior rodeo circuit. When I finally sold her, she still kept on giving because she kept Carter in school another semester.

Prescott, Prescott

Pete and I were sitting on the front porch of his house, having a beer. His new wife was inside, cooking supper with her mother. We were discussing the upcoming rodeo in Prescott when Pete's mother-in-law stuck her head out the door.

"Prescott, Prescott, that's all I hear! You ought to have Prescott up yore ass!" she hollered.

Pete didn't even look at her. He took a slow sip of his beer and replied, "Ain't room with all the other stuff you told me to stick up there!"

The Old Timer

The old timer worked with us at Tovreas, one of the best hands I've ever known. His horses were always well-trained, and he knew exactly where to be at the right time. He taught me a lot—some good, some bad. You see, he had a few vices: he was a drinker, gambler, womanizer, and just an all-around rounder.

One time, at a roping in Tucson at the Buckskin Bar (which had an arena out back), he matched us against another team in a five-steer roping. The other team was damn good at match ropings, but when it was all over, we'd won by a tenth of a second.

I was loading the horses while he went to collect the winnings. When he came back, he handed me a wad of cash.

"How much did we win?" I asked.

"A thousand a man," he replied.

"But I didn't have a thousand to gamble," I said.

"Neither did I," he smirked, "but they didn't know that when I matched 'em!"

We got out of town and laid low for a while after that!

Feed Yard Ropins

A bit of history on feed yard ropings: The first three or four were organized by Pfizer Pharmaceuticals, a popular outfit in the 1960s known for vaccines, antibiotics, and such. These ropings were held at Frank Powell's arena, located at 32nd Street and Southern in Phoenix, which was a hotspot for roping at the time.

They had a free barbecue, and the winners received a ton of feed supplement, along with gold buckles. In those days, buckles were a rare prize, and saddles were unheard of. At the first roping, there were about 50 teams, and it only grew from there.

Many people tried to get weekend jobs at feed yards just to qualify to enter. Only feed yard employees could compete, and you had to show proof when you entered with a pay stub. Usually, a PRCA member would be drafted to flag, and Frank Powell would supply the cattle. These were muley cattle, and the roping was a tie-down style—dally roping was unheard of back then; only the lily-white Californians did that!

I remember some of the winners from those ropings, but not the exact order. The Tovreas crew won the first four. Sam White, Pete Black, Gilbert Flores, A.D. Browning, and Buster Hall all earned Pfizer buckles. I didn't get one because, back then, I was the kid, and someone had to watch the yard at home. But as time passed and others began organizing feed yard ropings, I finally got my chance.

As my old friend, Weldon Rutledge, would say, "There will always be another roping, and we'll all be there!"

Bill Roer later produced a feed yard roping during his Rope-a-Thon in Laveen. Producers Cattle Feeders hosted one, as did AZL at the Hughes and Ganz feed yard in Queen Creek. By then, the event had turned into a dally roping.

Then, CALF magazine got involved and created the International Feed Yard Roping Association. They split the U.S. into regions, including Canada, and held qualifying ropings in each region. The top five teams in each category would go to the finals, which were initially held in Las Vegas, then moved indoors to Elko, Nevada.

After the third finals in Elko, I quit working feed yards and was no longer eligible to compete. But that's how it all started, and it was a lot of fun. There were a lot of great hands back then, both in the arena and at the feed yard. To name a few: Bill Magill, Johnny Rodriguez, Mike Benitas, Pablo Osuna, John Clem, and my old friend and partner, Joe Clem. Most of them are gone now, but they're not forgotten.

George Mason

I just got word that my old friend, George Mason—who was a stock contractor, brand inspector, and WWII hero—has passed. He must have been in his 90s. We will all miss him.

Years ago, when I was a kid and George was contracting rodeos, he had an old sorrel horse in his bareback string that was a real treat to watch. They always ran him last during the performance. He would generally buck off his rider, or when the rider got off, the old sorrel would run to the pickup man, stop, and stand stock still while they unsaddled him in the arena. They would then saddle him with a roping saddle and run the first steer in the team roping! A better tie-down horse was hard to find. You'd never know it was the same horse unless you were watching the bareback riding.

Hawkeye

Years ago, I left Maricopa at 3 in the morning, headed to Mormon Lake for the ropings there on the 4th of July. I left early because I was traveling by myself and wanted to be there in time for the first roping. At Cordes Junction, there used to be an all-night cafe called the Hub. I arrived early enough to stop for breakfast. As I pulled into the parking lot, I saw a big bonfire at the end with a lot of motorcycles parked around it. There were Hell's Angels types walking around the cafe and down by the bonfire. Two highway patrol cars were parked side by side, keeping an eye on the party.

I eased up as close to those guys as I could and parked, figuring they would keep the bikers away from my stuff while I ate. I unloaded my horse and tied him to the back of the trailer. As I walked toward the cafe, one of the patrolmen reassured me that my outfit would be fine.

When I got inside, I saw two bikers holding a third between them at the cash register, making him pay his bill. One apologized to the waitress and said their rude friend wouldn't be back. An old friend who lived nearby was there having breakfast, so we sat together, visited, and ate.

When I got back outside, there were no patrolmen in sight, and two bikers were sitting on the hood of my truck. Seeing no other way around it, I walked past, loaded my horse, and headed for the cab. As I passed the truck, I glanced in the back and noticed my bedroll and camp outfit seemed to be in place. As I reached the cab, the bikers slid off the truck and walked away. One looked back and said, "Your outfit's all there. Hawkeye said to watch it." Before I could ask who Hawkeye was, they were gone.

I went on to Mormon Lake, roped for three days, made a little money, and had a good time. Back home, it was work as usual—the same old feedlot grind.

About a month later, I was sick of my own cooking and decided to go to Maricopa to the Headquarters Cafe for supper and hit the bar next door afterward. As I walked into the cafe, I spotted a schoolmate of mine, someone I had played football with, sitting there eating supper. I slid into the booth with him, and we visited while he ate. He was a few years older than me but had always been a friend.

He was just finishing when my supper arrived, and I offered to buy him a drink afterward, but he said his "ale lady" was on the way to pick him up. Just then, a real attractive, long-legged blonde in biker leather walked up and asked, "Hawkeye, are you ready to go?" That's when I finally knew who Hawkeye was.

Fire!!

Years ago, if you were a rodeo hand in Arizona, during the Fourth of July weekend, you went to two places: Prescott or Mormon Lake. If you were really dedicated, you made both. Mormon Lake, just outside Flagstaff, had a steakhouse lodge with a bar, a roping arena, a few private cabins, and lots of camping space in the pines. For three or four days, from daylight to dark, they held a roping event. In Prescott, it was the world's oldest rodeo, with a great show, street dances on Whiskey Row, and all kinds of events. Many team ropers would enter Prescott, rope their steer, load up, and run the hour and a half to Mormon Lake. 500 teams was unheard of at most places, but not at Mormon Lake. Rufus Brown always furnished the steers—big, tough, hard-running steers that most ropers today would whine about, but back then, we were so damn dumb, we didn't know any better.

With so many ropers there and everyone camping out, it got crowded. So crowded, in fact, that if you needed to leave, it was almost impossible. You might have to get three or four people to break camp and move their rigs just so you could get to the road! Back then, motorhomes were unheard of, and living quarter trailers were rare. Most of us had a six-pack camper on a pickup with a two-horse trailer—maybe a canvas fly off one side for a little shade. Partner Joe and I had rigged our outfits so we could stretch a tarp between the two campers. It was real homey. We had a little camp table and kept a poker game going between go-rounds. There were loudspeakers strung in the trees all through camp, so you kept an ear cocked for a team number close to yours, giving you time to get ready. Some of those poker games got almost as rich as the ropings! Joe would sit back and braid headstalls and bridle reins to sell for entry fees and poker money. If you won something that day, you went to the steakhouse and ate that night, then danced and had a few drinks. If not, you kicked back in camp, drank your own beer, cooked a burger, and BS'd with your neighbor. Good times!

One year, right in the middle of the Saturday roping, someone hollered, "Fire!" We all looked up, and the lodge was smoking, flames licking out of the second-story windows! There was no fire department within 30 miles, and even if there had been, it couldn't get to the lodge because of all the trucks. The roping announcer said that anyone not roping needed to take their family and horses and climb the hill behind the arena to safety. The roping went on. The forest service showed up with some hotshots, trying to contain what they could. That hillside wasn't real safe—lots of big pine trees, dry as could be—and the lodge was putting out lots of sparks. There was no way to get your trucks out. Talk about gridlock! Some brave soul was running water from a garden hose onto the 1,000-gallon propane tank next to the lodge, flames licking the tank as he worked to keep it cool.

Pretty soon, the forest service told us to move back more because a slurry bomber was going to make a drop on the lodge. A lead plane passed over, then the bomber splattered the lodge with pink slurry—along with every truck, trailer, and unattended horse or roper! But the fire was out, and the roping never stopped. Just goes to show you the dedication of team ropers!

July Fourth

I spent the morning trying to come up with a cowboy story that would fit with today. I remember a lot of the Independence Days I spent at ropings, rodeos, and such. A few I spent at home or working, but I can't remember a single one that I wasn't proud to be an American cowboy. The story I'll tell you today shows the great lengths that cowboys will go through to celebrate the Fourth. And, in this case, I had an added incentive, as you'll see.

For six years, I was a member of the Arizona National Guard.

This one year, some fool scheduled our summer camp at Fort Irwin outside of Barstow, California, over the Fourth of July weekend!! I had partners at Mormon Lake counting on me to be there!! (Not to mention me counting on being there!) When I left on the convoy to Barstow, I entrusted my truck, trailer, and horse to a cute brunette I was dating. I had no idea how we'd do it, but I told her we were going to Mormon Lake the next weekend!!

Thursday afternoon, I found a ride to Phoenix from Barstow. I called my dolly and told her to have the truck packed, gassed, and ole Rabbit in the trailer by Friday afternoon, and we'd hit the trail to Flagstaff. If all worked out, we'd be at Mormon Lake Saturday morning for the first roping.

Sure enough, I landed at dolly's doorstep about 4 p.m. Friday, stepped out of one crowded car into that Ford rodeo rig, and we scorched the road to Mormon Lake. And, sure enough, we were roping Saturday. Didn't win a dime, but partied and danced, then got a good night's sleep in preparation for Sunday's roping. Roped Sunday morning, blew out in the first round, loaded up, and headed back to Phoenix to catch my ride back to Barstow. Six of us packed into a car, headed back. The driver got tired, so he let some other cannon cocker drive.

We all went to sleep, and a while later the driver woke us to tell us he was lost!!! We were in San Bernardino!!! Fool missed Barstow!!! We were going to be AWOL!!! Got turned around, drove like hell back the way we came, rolled into the barracks, ran through, changed clothes, and ran out the back door into formation just in time to hear our names called in roll.

All that, and it was worth every minute of the trip!! Dolly took care of ole Rabbit, the Ford, and when I got back from summer camp, made a lifelong commitment to go down the road with me!!! She's still here, and why I don't know, but every Fourth, I think of that trip. It's hell to get old, but this country just gets better and better with each birthday. Yeah, we got problems, but nothing can't be fixed.

Where else on Earth can a young man and woman do what we did?

The All-Girl Ropin'

Years ago, the girl rodeo contestants needed to raise some money for a worthy cause of some sort—I don't remember what. Since I was a certified judge/flagman for their barrel races, I was invited to judge this event. Never could turn down a smiling blonde. This event was held at Frank Powell's arena at 36th and Southern in Phoenix. Frank furnished the cattle for all kinds of fun events. A calf dressing event, where a three-girl team roped and put a pair of bloomers on a calf; an all-girl roping; a ribbon roping, where a male roper would rope a calf, and the lady would pull a ribbon off the tail of the calf and race back to the finish line. Lots of fun. Lots of beer consumed. Which led us to the last event: a Jeep roping. A local car dealer had donated the use of a brand-new Jeep for the event. The Jeep was backed into the header's box. A driver, a roper, and two girls in the back loaded up. A calf was turned out, the driver roared up to the calf, the roper caught the calf, and tied the rope to the roll bar, a la John Wayne in *Hatari*! The girls jumped out and tied the calf to get a time.

Great fun!! Now this Jeep was yellow, with a chrome bumper and tuck-and-roll upholstery, fancy, powered by a 283 Chevy engine. This thing was as hot as it looked!!!

All went well until Gene Ray, Tommy, and their two gals were up.

Now Gene and Tommy were two of the best ropers anywhere, bar none. But they were also champion beer drinkers!! When the gate opened, Gene Ray was driving and started running that yellow Jeep through the gears. Tommy was standing up to the roll bar, swinging his twine in anticipation of a quick catch. The girls in the back cheering them on!! The calf wasn't going for this deal at all and made a beeline for the left fence, then made a sharp right and headed down the arena for home. When Gene got to the left fence, he forgot to make that right-hand turn!! The Jeep hit a light pole, dead center, in third gear. Tommy flew over the roll bar and made contact with the same light pole!! The two girls in the back slammed into the seats!! That stopped the cheering. Two bloody noses, Tommy out cold, and Gene Ray walked away untouched, looking for a beer!!! That pretty little Jeep had a permanent crease right dead center, all the way back to the driver's seat!! I don't know who, if anyone, paid for that Jeep, but I heard later that the car dealer almost lost his religion over that deal!!

Mike

Mike could rope. I haven't seen him in years, but I'll bet he can still rope, if he's alive. You see, Mike didn't just sip at life—he ran against it with a funnel in his mouth. He was a good hand with horses, a damn good cowboy, and a hell of a horseshoer. But he was also doing his best to run out his string as fast as he could. A lot of people didn't like Mike, but we got along well. We traveled together, roped together, partied together—but Mike sure could stir the pot.

Once, on our way home from a roping, we stopped at a Circle K for a little octane (for us, not the truck). As we were walking across the parking lot, a popular song at the time was playing on the store's sound system. It was Ray Stevens' "The Streak." Mike just kind of did a shuffle and sashayed around an old lady on the way to her car. She bristled up and said, "What is this?" Mike, without missing a beat, replied, "This is a streak" and started peeling off his clothes!

I went inside for the beer while he put his clothes back on. As we drove off, a cop was pulling into the parking lot. Nobody ever said anything, but I had to keep an eye on Mike for a while.

Mike was prone to disappear for months at a time, but he was a good enough hand that when he did show up, he'd get hired on no problem. We were practicing one evening in May when his header missed a steer. Mike spurred up and, using the fence as a hazer, got down on the steer. Now, ANYBODY who bulldogs knows you don't do that. Sure enough, Mike houlihaned the steer and broke his leg—not the steer, Mike!

When the doc was done, Mike had a cast from his ankle to his crotch. It was a month and a half until the Fourth of July. The doctor told him not to plan on going to the rodeo. Well, you guessed it—Mike went anyway. He cut the cast off and would freeze the leg before he roped. And wouldn't you know it, he won a wagonload of money! A month later, he seemed just fine except for the little hop he had when he walked. But he said that was okay—the girls thought it was sexy!

Rodeos and Ropings

Some of my earliest memories of rodeos and ropings go back to the old Phoenix Jaycee Rodeo, held at the fairgrounds in Phoenix. I couldn't have been more than five or six when my dad first took me there. The old concrete stadium was packed, as it always was every time we went after that. My dad was a big fan of rodeo. He knew all the contestants, what they competed in, where they came from, and who the world champions were. I never realized he kept track of all that since he didn't compete himself. He could rope, and rope well, but never entered any contests. Some of the best times I had as a kid were going to the rodeos with him.

When the fair commission built the coliseum at the fairgrounds, we attended a lot of rodeos and roping events there. I remember watching Dale Smith and Bill Hamilton in a match calf roping competition—ten head for $1,000 a side. Big money in those days. I think Hamilton won that one. As a few years passed, I started competing in team ropings at that venue. It was a little tight for tie-down ropings, but you could dally rope without too much trouble. Back then, that old barn was the only indoor facility in Arizona. I showed horses there, roped there, and watched many great rodeo contestants.

As the years passed, the Jaycee Rodeo faded away, though I never really knew why. I miss it to this day. Another rodeo that disappeared was the Chandler Sheriff's Posse Rodeo, a great outdoor event. I remember watching the bucking horse "War Paint" there. And yes, he did get his man.

One night, I was at a roping at Frank Powell's arena at 36th and Southern. I was feeling a bit cocky, as I'd been on a good roll, and a couple of pretty girls were following me around to the ropings. Frank came over and asked if I had all my partners, as there was a guy who needed a header. He was the world champion bull rider. I said, "So what? Can he rope?" I didn't rope with that world champion bull rider, but the guys who did won the roping with him. Now, that was a weekend pumpkin roller, but it was as important to Larry Mahan as winning the world in bull riding. Go figure. What kind of dummy am I?

As the years went by, I was fortunate enough to compete at some great venues, both indoors and out. I had the opportunity to meet and socialize with world champions and also-rans. One of the classiest gentlemen I ever met was world champion team roper John Miller. A pure gentleman, always the same with everyone, whether you were a beginner or a pro. He was well mounted at all times and treated his horses as athletes and partners, always giving them credit for his success. I got to know John a little better in later years when we both attended junior rodeos with our kids. One of his friends was Ace Berry, who went to the NFR numerous times as a bareback rider AND a heeler for John. Not many contestants could do both! Ace was a class act too. Both of those fellas were raised by movie actor and world champion team roper Ben Johnson. Despite all Ben did to help him, John made it on his own. I believe John's kids are still roping today, and though I haven't seen him in a long time, I'd bet he's still the class act he was back then.

One of my earliest memories of rodeo was being at the Phoenix Rodeo, watching Ben Johnson rope. We were sitting pretty high in the stands, but to this day, I can still hear the rope making a cracking sound when Ben roped those horns. Then there was Wilber Plaugher, who clowned and fought bulls. When bulldogging came around, Wilber would climb on a horse in his clown gear and dog a steer—not as a joke, but as a serious competitor. I believe he got a check almost everywhere he went.

Well, there it is. It's been a great ride, and I've met some great folks along the way. I hope to meet more!

Foot Race

In the early days of civilization, foot racing was a popular form of entertainment. It made a brief resurgence in the early 70s within the rodeo and jackpot roping community. The big name at the time was Ray. Fresh back from Vietnam, with a bit of money in his pocket and a love for gambling, Ray became the one to beat.

Before I met him, he had already outrun the backfield of the ASU football team and was challenging anyone with cash in hand. As Ray outran more and more people, it became harder to find a worthy opponent. So, he started giving up ground at the start.

His favorite race was the length of a roping arena. He'd give his opponent a head start—about a third of the arena—and then, in the catch pen, the race would begin. Ray had to jump the fence into the arena and chase down his opposition. A few of those races were close—real close—but I never knew him to lose.

At the Mormon Lake Fourth of July roping, Ray was trying to get a match-up. No takers. He gave up half the arena, still no takers. In desperation, he offered to smoke a pack of cigarettes and drink a six-pack of beer before the race, but still, no one bit. Finally, he offered to match his new wife against any other woman there. When no one took him up on that, he raised the stakes and offered to race his six-month-old son against any other kid his age in a crawling contest. No takers on that, either.

The last race I saw Ray run nearly did him in. We were at the old 35th and Baseline Arena when somehow; he ended up matched against Bill Roer in a race. Bill was in his 60s, while Ray was in his mid-30s. Bill was a hell of an athlete for his age and loved to gamble. The terms were: Ray started in the catch pen, lying flat on his belly, while Bill got a two-thirds head start but had to run backwards. The bet was for a thousand dollars each.

When the flag dropped, Bill started trotting backward, watching Ray leap over the fence flat-footed before charging after him like a bat out of hell. As Bill neared the finish line, those of us who had bet against him could see our money flying away. It seemed impossible for Ray to make up the distance—Bill was running backwards as fast as some people ran forwards! Just as Bill was within reach of the finish line, he fell. It knocked the wind out of him, and he lay there, wheezing for air, as Ray passed him.

All Bill had to do was reach back and touch the finish line to win, but he later told me he wasn't sure where he was. As far as I know, that was the last footrace after that one, and Ray swore he'd never gamble with Bill Roer again.

Match Ropins

At one time, match ropins were a popular event. "I'll bet X amount I can out-rope ya!" I've seen as many as three or four teams set up a match for as little as $50 a man, with the winner taking it all. It takes a different mindset to do that kind of roping. At a rodeo, you rope each go-round as fast as you can. At a jackpot, you try to rope all your cattle and win the average. But in a match roping, you rope just a little better than the other guy, but not the absolute best you can. You've got to pay attention to what the other team is doing, what you're doing, and know the cattle by their first names!

There've been plenty of match ropins in the calf roping world, and it's still popular in states where they rope lots of calves. Team roping matches, however, have kind of fallen out of favor in Arizona. I don't really know why—could be a lot of reasons.

The first match roping I competed in was in Tucson. My partner was an old gambler, roper, pool player, and down-right scoundrel, but he knew how to match rope. We won the match, and if I'd known what we were roping for, I might have choked—but he didn't tell me. What he did tell me was what the steer was like, where to rope him, and how to handle him. We won by just a few tenths of a second, but we could have won by more. But we didn't show them everything we had. It was kind of like hustling pool. We matched those boys a couple more times before they gave up. If we'd shown all our cards at once, all we'd have gotten was the first match, and no one else would have matched us after that. I didn't know this at the time, but I learned as we went along.

Years later, we belonged to a roping club, and some of the members thought it would be fun to have a match roping after the Saturday night roping. After about six weeks, those same guys were wanting to ban the matches. My partner at the time was a slick header who could get the rope out of his hand pretty quick, but he didn't always think ahead. The last match we had was a two-header. There were four teams entered. I don't remember the exact amount we roped for, but it wasn't a lot—maybe $25 a man.

I had a little blue roan heel horse at the time who was as quick as any horse I've ever ridden and could stop on a dime. Judd turned our first steer just across the line, and the clock stopped at 5 flat. The other teams were in the 7-second range, so I knew we had a lot of leeway, but Judd didn't see it that way. On the second steer, he turned even quicker. I tracked the steer for four jumps and roped him by two feet—6 flat! At the time, that was an arena record for two steers. The other teams went long, and we beat them by a big margin. By the next roping, they had banned matches.

Don't get me wrong, I lost a lot of match ropins— probably as many as I won—but I never complained about someone roping better than me. I just went home, practiced harder, or tried to make my horse better. Not so today. Everyone's handicapped, so those who don't want to work as hard as someone else still have a chance to win their money back. I hate whiners and those with weak hearts.

Jingle Bells

When I was in high school, I caught the horse show bug. As we all know, high school boys don't have much common sense, and I was no exception. I had bred a mare to an Appaloosa stud, and the result was a wild-colored, blanket-hipped colt. By the time I was a sophomore, I had that horse broke to do just about everything you could think of. Naturally, you could rope off him. He wasn't a bad western pleasure horse, trail courses were a piece of cake, and reining was just plain boring. We won every 4-H class available, so we moved on to the breed shows. We were placing everywhere we went, even winning some.

One of my fellow competitors made a wisecrack about the only thing we hadn't done was a costume class. In the Appaloosa world, this involved dressing up like an Indian and riding around the ring showing off both how well-broke your horse was and how authentic your costume looked.

I mentioned this to my mom, and she got to work. Without the internet back then, I went to the library and grabbed a book on the Nez Perce tribe—the people who raised the Appaloosa horses before the breed was influenced by draft horses. I learned that the Nez Perce were fond of bells on their clothes, horses, and anything else they could tie them to. So, I bought a big string of jingle bells and had my mom sew them all over the costume.

Before the class entered the ring, I braided a bunch more bells into my horse's mane and tail.

Since I had never shown in a costume class before, I paid close attention to a few that took place at previous shows. A wise old trainer, who took a liking to me, gave me a piece of advice: "Always be the first in the ring or the last. The judge looks at those the hardest."

So, I hung back in the shadows until the others entered. When the ring was full, I spurred my horse into a full run, charging in with all those bells jingling like Santa Claus on Christmas Eve. I wore a war bridle on my pony, and the feathers nearly dragged the ground. As I passed each competitor, I heard the crowd roar. I figured they were just impressed with my great, authentic costume. But as I lapped the arena, I noticed no one else was on horseback. Some were chasing their horses, which had bolted to the far end of the arena. The crowd was laughing so hard that the loudspeaker was barely audible.

Casey Darnel, the judge, was standing in the middle of the ring, crooking his finger at me. I slowed to a trot and rode over to him.

"Just wait here, Kid," he told me. "Let those other folks catch their horses so I can figure out who wins second and third."

That was the end of my costume class career. By the following year, I'd outgrown both the costume and my desire to compete in that class. Besides, if I told anyone I was entering, no one else would dare!

www.ingramcontent.com/pod-product-compliance
Lightning Source LLC
Chambersburg PA
CBHW071620150726
48000CB00004B/1802